Why make a website?

There are lots of reasons to make a website. Maybe you want to tell the world about yourself, or provide a place where friends and family can catch up on what you're doing. Perhaps you run a local club and want a calendar of events and a forum where members can chat, ask questions or offer advice. Alternatively, you might want to promote your small business to attract more custom.

The good news is that you don't need to be an expert in web design to build a website that's both attractive and user-friendly. These days, it's easier than ever to make your online presence felt, thanks to free online tools that let you choose a template and replace the example words and pictures with your own.

If you want to know how to create a stunning website with dynamic features such as video, interactive maps and photo galleries, this book is for you, regardless of experience. It's also for anyone who wants to know how to build a website the *right* way.

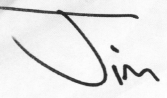

Jim Martin, Editor
jim_martin@dennis.co.uk

Contents

CHAPTER 5

Looking good

Making a site with an attractive design isn't simple, but armed with these tips, your site can rival the best-looking examples

CHAPTER 6

Content management

Find out how to install the WordPress blogging tool on your site and how the Joomla content management system works

CHAPTER 7

Adding sparkle

There are many ways to make your site more exciting, including adding video, weather forecasts or even a community forum

CHAPTER 8

Finishing touches

Check your site for any legal problems, include adverts to earn cash and find out how many visitors your site is attracting

CHAPTER 9

Advanced projects

Create and use web applications to show photo galleries and Google Maps. Plus, learn how to create boxes with round corners

Getting started

You've decided to create your own website, and your head is buzzing with ideas about what will be on it and how it will look. However, first you need to decide where to host your site. You're not going to want to host it on your PC at home, as the site will be unavailable when you switch off the computer. Instead, you need a web-hosting provider. In this chapter, we'll compare the most popular options.

You'll want your site to have a memorable address such as www.bradpitt.com rather than http://bradpitt. geocities.com, so we'll show you how to register a domain name. We'll also compare a variety of web-creation programs and design software. And if you're really pushed for time, we'll even show you how to create a website in just 30 minutes.

Free web hosting

Before you can start on your website, you need a good web-hosting service. We look at those that will serve your site for free

Running a complex and popular website usually comes with financial burdens, but creating and maintaining an internet presence needn't be a bank-breaking endeavour. One of the best ways to keep initial costs down is to opt for a free hosting service. These services provide web space for you to store your site, although they often impose some restrictions.

The most significant of these is the domain name. Free web-hosting services don't provide you with your own domain name. This means that, while you may be after www.redcotbarn.co.uk, you may have to make do with http://sites.google.com/site/redcotbarn or www.redcot-barn.freehost.co.uk.

This isn't necessarily a problem if you're building a website as a hobby, but it's not ideal if you want to appear more professional. Some free web-hosting services allow you to use your own domain name, but you'll have to buy this separately, often for a yearly fee. This can then redirect users to your free hosting package, so a visitor typing www.redcotbarn.co.uk into their browser actually ends up at a different website, such as www.freehost.co.uk/redcotbarn. You can find more on buying and managing domain names on page 16.

Free web-hosting services tend to have tight bandwidth restrictions and come with a small amount of web space. This limits what you can put on your website

Free web-hosting packages

Package	URL	Space	Monthly bandwidth	Email accounts
Free Virtual Servers	www.freevirtualservers.com	100MB	100MB	10
Heart Internet	www.heartinternet.co.uk	2.5GB	100MB	1,000
BraveNet.com	www.bravenet.com	50MB	1.5GB	No
NetFirms	www.netfirms.com	25MB	1GB	Yes
Mysite.com	www.mysite.com	50MB (250KB file limit)	1GB	No
One.com	www.one.com	3GB	Unlimited	Unlimited
Free-space	www.free-space.net	200MB	2GB	5
Google Sites	http://sites.google.com	10GB	N/A	Free Gmail account
Yahoo! GeoCities	www.geocities.com	15MB	4.2MB/hour	N/A
350 Pages	www.350.com	20MB or 15 pages	1GB	No

Please note: Details correct at time of going to press

and how many people can visit. One way to reduce the effect of these limits is to store disk-hungry content such as photos and videos elsewhere. YouTube can host your videos, while a photo service such as Flickr (www.flickr.com) can store images. Find out how to embed YouTube videos in your web pages on page 100.

While some hosting providers offer generous bandwidth limits and plentiful web space, they may lack advanced features such as MySQL databases and support for scripting languages such as PHP and Perl. This may not matter at first, but as your ambitions grow and your website expands, you may wish to add a blog or keep a customer database. Turn to Chapter 9 for examples of what these technologies can offer. Another disadvantage of a free service is that File Transfer Protocol (FTP) access to your site may be limited. This means you must upload files using a proprietary web interface, perhaps one file at a time, which can be a real aggravation if you have a large website with lots of files.

You will probably also have to put up with some form of external advertising on your website if you choose free hosting. Adverts are usually placed at the side or bottom of each web page. Often the only way to avoid them is to pay a fee for your account.

TWO APPROACHES TO FREEDOM

Google Sites is an example of a completely free service. All you need is a Google account, which is also free. Google Sites allows you to create a basic website using templates you can modify. You get 10GB of dedicated storage to play with, and a limited range of tools. You can also add gadgets such as clocks, search bars and games.

Left: One.com's free hosting package is a cut above the rest, but you have to pay a one-off £12 setup fee

It's a fast way to get a personal website, but it's not suitable for a small business and it won't be easy to reuse the content or expand your site beyond the initial format if you want to make it bigger and better later.

One.com's free hosting package provides a more traditional and complete hosting service. You get 3GB of storage space for your web pages, images and other content, and (amazingly) unlimited bandwidth. This is coupled with an unlimited number of email accounts, FTP access and support for MySQL databases, and a handful of scripting languages such as PHP and ASP. It's also easier to scale up from this kind of website simply by upgrading your account. It's not strictly free – you pay a setup fee of £12 – but it's still excellent value. The package includes your own domain name, which you can use for a year, after which you must pay to keep it. This option is more suitable for burgeoning business websites.

Adverts	FTP access	Use own domain name?	Site-builder tools	Example URL	In a nutshell
No	Yes	Yes	Yes	www.redcotbarn.co.uk	Domain name required. SQL database. No sub domains
No	Yes	Yes	No	www.redcotbarn.co.uk	Domain name required
Yes	Yes	Yes	Yes	www.redcotbarn.bravehosts.com	Google advertising
Yes	Yes	Yes	Yes	http://redcotbarn.netfirms.com	Perl and FrontPage support
Yes	No	Yes	No	http://redcotbarn.4t.com	No scripting, SQL or FTP access
No	Yes	Yes	Yes	www.redcotbarn.co.uk	Free domain name for the first year, £12 setup fee
No	Yes	Yes	Yes	www.redcotbarn.co.uk	Domain name required
Yes	No	No	Yes	http://sites.google.com/site/redcotbarn	Basic web building with templates. Can't edit HTML
Yes	No	No	Yes	www.geocities.com/redcotbarn	Intrusive advertising
Yes	No	Yes	Yes	www.redcotbarn.350.com	Template based. Can't edit HTML. Unintrusive ads

Web-hosting packages

There's a dizzying choice of hosting providers out there. Here we look at the most popular paid-for packages to make choosing a host easier

- Get your own unique domain name for your website
- Get unlimited bandwidth for unlimited visitors to your site
- Get advanced features such as databases and scripting languages

If you've tried to create a website using the free web space that came with your broadband package – or you've tried out some of the free hosting services we mentioned on page 10 – you'll already know the main drawbacks. Quite apart from the fact that your website's address isn't particularly personal or memorable, you may also want faster server speeds, more space and extras such as database access and scripting services that let you create a more dynamic site.

Hosting packages offer a set amount of storage and a bandwidth limit – the amount of data that can be downloaded from your site – for a monthly fee. You should work out how much space and bandwidth you'll need. Most hosting companies will slow down your connection or charge you extra if you exceed your monthly bandwidth, rather than shutting your site down.

Some packages include a domain name, so you can choose something short and memorable such as

Web-hosting packages

Package	URL	Monthly price including VAT	Extra costs	Space
Eukhost Gold	www.eukhost.com	£4.60	None	5GB
Heart Internet Starter Professional	www.heartinternet.co.uk	£2.49	£10 setup fee	5GB
1&1 Home	www.1&1.co.uk	£4.99	None	1.5GB
eHosting eS Silver	www.ehosting.com	£4.49	None	2.5GB
Fasthosts Home	www.fasthosts.co.uk	£3.99	None	1.5GB
Netcetera One	www.netcetera.co.uk	£6.00	None	5GB
Payasyouhost Standard	www.payasyouhost.co.uk	£4.69	None	250MB
UK2.NET Home	www.uk2.net	£4.17	None	3GB
Zen Internet Bronze	www.zen.co.uk	£3.99	None	1GB
WebEden Lite	www.webeden.co.uk	£2.69	None	50MB
One.com 10GB	www.one.com	£2.23	£12 setup fee	10GB
Mr Site Takeaway Website Standard	www.mrsite.com	£2.50	None	150MB

Please note: Details correct at time of going to press

TIP

Most services have transparent costs, but watch out for start-up fees or domain registration charges, which may not be included in the service's advertised monthly price.

www.redcotbarn.co.uk. If you want a package that doesn't come with a domain, there are several in the table below, or you can turn to page 16 to find out how and where to buy one. Email accounts are usually included with the package, along with tools to help you manage your site. Some packages come with complete website-creation tools (see page 18), but others don't. Some support Microsoft FrontPage extensions, which means you can design a website in FrontPage and publish it directly to your hosting package from your desktop.

DECISIONS, DECISIONS

One important decision you will need to make is whether to opt for Linux- or Windows-based servers. This will be influenced by your choice of web-design application (see pages 24-27) or scripting language, and the advanced features you want. If you want a dynamic site that creates web pages on demand, you need a combination of a scripting language and a database. The most popular combination is MySQL for the database, which holds the content, and the PHP scripting language, which extracts content from the database. You can use a database for many things, such as a chat forum (see page 108) or a content management system (see page 94). Each function usually needs its own database, so plan your needs from the outset and choose a package with sufficient databases.

Reliability is also important, as you don't want your site to disappear for days on end. Look for a provider's

Left: When choosing a hosting package, make sure it has all the features you need

'guaranteed uptime', which tells you the percentage of time the server remains accessible online. Even an uptime of 99.9 per cent could mean your site is inaccessible for 40 minutes every month. It may be worth paying for this level of uptime if you earn money from your website. You can also check forums to see how other users rate a particular company for technical support.

The table below provides a summary of some of the most popular and best-value web-hosting packages, along with their key features. For the latest prices, you should visit the web addresses shown in the table.

Bandwidth limit	Email account	Operating system	Domain name included?	Website creation tools	Scripts	MySQL database slots
50GB	Unlimited	Linux	Yes	Yes	PHP, Perl, CGI, Ruby	Unlimited
30GB	1,000	Linux	No	No	PHP, Perl, Python, ASP, Ruby	None
20GB	400	Linux	Yes	Limited	CGI	None
25GB	100	Linux or Windows	Yes	No	PHP, Perl, ASP	2
Unlimited	5 advanced, 200 standard	Linux or Windows	Yes	Yes	PHP, Perl, ASP, Python	None
Unlimited	1,000	Windows	No	No	PHP, Perl, ASP, ASP.NET, AJAX	1x 50MB
1.5GB	Unlimited	Linux	No	No	PHP, Perl, ASP, CGI	Unlimited
100GB	50	Linux	Yes	Yes	PHP, Perl, ASP, CGI, Ruby	1
3GB	10	Linux	No	No	PHP, Perl	3
6GB	No	Not stated	No	Yes	None	None
Unlimited	Unlimited	Linux	Yes	Yes	PHP, ASP	1
2GB	20	Not stated	Yes	Yes	JavaScript	None

Take advantage of our fantastic web hosting offer today!

Whether you're a home user, an internet professional, or a business
we have a web hosting package to suit you.
So buy now pay half price
for the first 3 months!

Half price web hosting

Great value packages to suit everyone's hosting needs.

From **£1.99** ~~£3.99~~ pm

Added features

Easy website builder, blog tools, images, email services and much more absolutely free.

Unlimited bandwidth

We don't restrict your website traffic or charge you extra.

24/7 UK HELPLINE
INCLUDED WITH ALL HOSTING PACKAGES

- UK based in-house call centre
- Telephone and email support
- Experts on hand whenever you need them

fasthosts.co.uk
Phone 0870 888 3517

All prices exclude VAT

Cracking package

More space, more email & more traffic with

Half price web hosting

From

£1.99 ~~£3.99~~

Home Web hosting

Free Unlimited bandwidth
1.5 GB UK web space

- **FREE** Website builder
- **FREE** Instant blog
- **FREE** £50 MSN adCenter voucher
- Graphical website statistics
- 5 Advanced mailboxes
- Spam & virus protected email

£1.99 ~~£3.99~~ pm

Developer Web hosting

Free Unlimited bandwidth
4 GB UK web space

- **FREE** Website builder
- **FREE** Instant blog
- **FREE** £50 MSN adCenter voucher
- ASP.NET 2.0 with AJAX
- ASP, PHP & Perl CGI scripting
- SSL secure web space
- Password protected folders
- 10 Advanced mailboxes
- Spam & virus protected email

£3.99 ~~£7.99~~ pm

Business Web hosting

Free Unlimited bandwidth
10 GB UK web space

- **FREE** Website builder
- **FREE** Outlook software
- **FREE** £50 MSN adCenter voucher
- Microsoft Exchange email
- Unlimited POP3/IMAP mailboxes
- 15 Advanced mailboxes
- Load balanced web servers
- Powerful search engine tools
- ASP.NET 2.0 with AJAX
- ASP, PHP & Perl CGI scripting
- MS SQL or MySQL database
- SSL secure web space

£7.99 ~~£15.99~~ pm

fasthosts

Buying a domain name

For a professional appearance, your website needs its own unique web address, or domain name. Here's how to get one

A domain name is a unique name for your website. It's more than just an address that enables people to find your site, though. It's a brand, and something to be remembered by. It's important to choose the right domain name for your website if you want to entice people to visit and then keep coming back.

There are two important things to consider when choosing a domain name. First, your chosen name should be both memorable and relevant to the content of your site. There's little point in choosing www.jimsphotos.com if your name isn't Jim and you haven't got any photos to show. Your choice of domain name should also make it easier for people to find you. If you run a book club in Oxford, people might guess at www.oxfordbookclub.com if they're not sure of the exact address, so it makes sense to register this domain.

Right: To see if a domain name is available to register, visit www.who.is and type in the name you want to register, excluding the 'www.' part

Access denied

Some domain names can turn out to be more trouble than they're worth. An example is a UK family that decided to register www.narnia.mobi in 2006 for their son, who is a huge fan of the CS Lewis books. However, now that more people are accessing websites from mobile devices, companies are beginning to register .mobi domains, which they see as theirs. Sure enough, the administrators of the estate of CS Lewis took the family to court and successfully won the right to the domain name.

Similarly, it's inadvisable to register a domain that sounds like another successful site. A few years ago, a student named Mike Rowe registered the domain www.mikerowesoft.com but ended up having to hand it over to Microsoft. Companies want to protect their trademarks, and you may find yourself the subject of legal proceedings if you do anything that might infringe them.

Domain names come in various types dictated by their endings. The most common ending for UK-based sites is .co.uk, but there is nothing to stop you registering a .org or .net extension, or even a more exotic .info, .me or .tv.

All .co.uk domain names are managed by Nominet, a not-for-profit company established to oversee the .uk top-level domain (TLD). You can buy a domain name directly from Nominet, but the company recommends that you use a licensed registrar. When you consider that buying a domain from Nominet costs around £80 for two years, it makes sense to follow this advice: buying the same domain through a registrar should cost under £10.

Most web-hosting providers also act as registrars and, although you are not obliged to buy the domain from your chosen host, it's far more convenient to do so. Prices vary between registrar services, though, so it could be worth shopping around before you buy.

Plenty of companies on the internet will register a domain name on your behalf, and you can also use these services to find out whether or not your desired domain name is available. Bear in mind that there's little chance of general, popular names being available, such as www.johnsmith.co.uk or www.karateclub.com. However, more descriptive names such as www.swaffham-karate.com or www.martinaccountants.co.uk may well be.

A NAME YOU CAN TRUST

If the particular domain name you want is unavailable, you have a number of options. You don't necessarily have to think of another name. Instead, you could find out if the same domain name is available with a different ending, such as .info or .biz. Of course, this means that another website will have a similar domain to your own, which could cause confusion. An alternative for those

who simply must have a certain name is to find out who currently owns the domain name and try to buy it. Enter the URL into a browser's address bar and look at the website that appears. If it's related to the domain name, you may have an uphill struggle, but if you are directed to a holding page with contact information, there's a good chance you will be able to negotiate a purchase.

Once you have bought your domain name, you must link it to your website. These are two entirely separate entities. A website is a collection of pages about a particular subject that's stored on a server, while the domain name is the information used to find those pages – a bit like a postcode. When www.redcotbarn.co.uk is entered in a web browser, it's crucial that the visitor arrives at the Redcot Barn website.

When you sign up for a web-hosting package, you'll usually be given the option to search for a new domain to buy, or to associate the web space with a domain you already own. This is a straightforward process. Simply follow the step-by-step instructions provided by your host (see our walkthrough on page 20 for an example).

Some hosting packages (free ones in particular) offer the chance to create a subdomain under the host's name, such as redcotbarn.freehost.co.uk. This can be useful for creating multiple websites. For example, we could establish http://bookings.redcotbarn.co.uk for the booking system.

FORWARD THINKING

Even if your website is hosted by a free service that doesn't allow personal domain names, you can use a domain forwarding service to associate your own domain with your website. This means that even if the Redcot Barn website's URL is www.redcotbarn.freehost.co.uk, you could buy the domain www.redcotbarn.co.uk and automatically forward visitors who type in this URL to the one at the free host. This service is usually provided for free or for a nominal fee. Again, if you require this service, shop around before you buy your domain name.

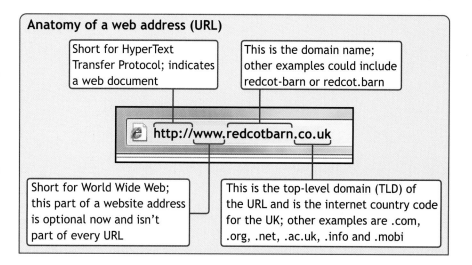

Anatomy of a web address (URL)

Short for HyperText Transfer Protocol; indicates a web document

This is the domain name; other examples could include redcot-barn or redcot.barn

http://www.redcotbarn.co.uk

Short for World Wide Web; this part of a website address is optional now and isn't part of every URL

This is the top-level domain (TLD) of the URL and is the internet country code for the UK; other examples are .com, .org, .net, .ac.uk, .info and .mobi

HTML editors and site-builder tools

Whether you want to get hands-on with HTML code or you need more wizard-based help, there are many tools to assist in building your site

BENEFITS ●●●

- Colour-coded HTML editors make it much easier to work with code than Windows' Notepad
- Site-builder tools do all the hard work for you

Once you've registered a domain name and associated it with a hosting package, you're ready to start building a website. You will achieve the best results if you build your site by hand. We'll show you exactly how to do this over the following chapters, but it makes sense to consider the options on offer from your hosting provider, as well as any tools you may already have or can download.

When you surf the internet, you use your web browser – and the power of your computer – to download and convert HTML files into the visual, aural and textual content you see on the screen. At its simplest, HTML is plain-English programming code that contains the textual content, page structure and instructions that

determine how your browser should display the web page, as well as links to other pages.

If you click the View menu option in Internet Explorer or Mozilla Firefox and select Source, you can see the code for the web page you're viewing. You don't need to know how HTML works or how to write your own because the site-builder tools here and the web-design software on page 24-27 enable you to create complex sites without ever seeing HTML code.

However, HTML is easy to understand, ands if you take the time to learn it, you will be better equipped for the ongoing development of your site (see Chapter 3). At the very least, it will help you to appreciate the underlying structure of web pages.

TAKE NOTE

HTML code can be written in an application as basic as Windows Notepad. However, although many of the examples in the following chapters can be followed using Notepad, we recommend using a dedicated editor instead. This will help you get to grips with HTML code and write it yourself. An HTML editor highlights the tags (the elements that define how content appears) in different colours, numbers each line and can insert tags for you, making the HTML easier to read and create.

Notepad2 (www.flos-freeware.ch) is a free, lightweight editor that includes syntax highlighting for a number of programming languages, including HTML. This separates your content from the instruction tabs that tell browsers what to do. Arachnophilia (www.arachnoid.com/arachnophilia) is a more comprehensive free editor. When you create a new HTML file, the basic structure is already in place and you simply add the content, while formatting and structure tags are just a click away.

Word-processing applications such as Microsoft Word and OpenOffice are also potential HTML editors. Both allow you to save a document as a web page, so they can

Below: Notepad2 is a free tool for creating HTML code that's easy to read

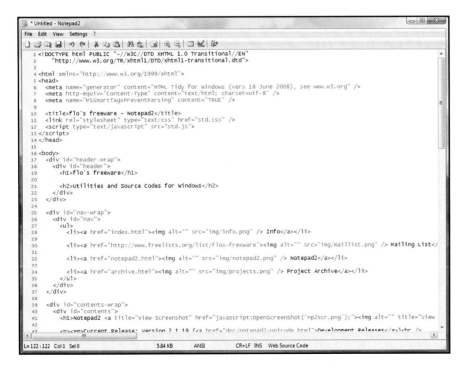

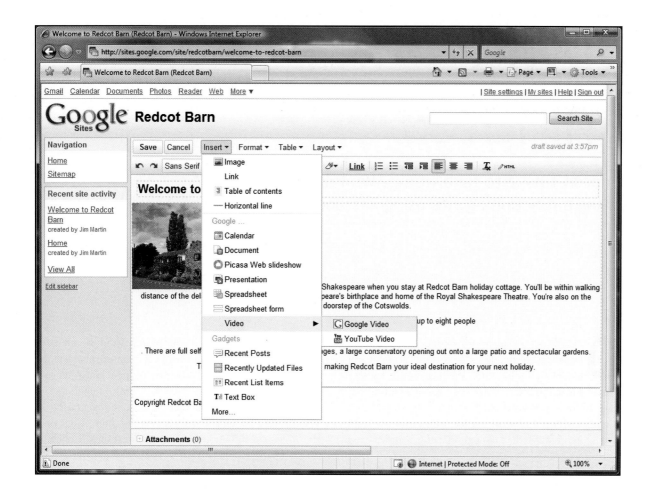

create an HTML file and a folder that contains all the images on your page. You can combine the table function with inserted images and formatting to create reasonably complex HTML pages.

FREEDOM RULES

Almost all web hosts offer some form of site-building tools to help you get your website off the drawing board and on to the internet. Even many free hosting accounts provide limited access to site-building tools. At their most basic, these provide templates that give you varying degrees of freedom over the final look of the page. This template approach means you can quickly get a presentable website up and running.

Yahoo!'s free GeoCities web hosting provides more freedom while still adhering to the template formula, allowing you to rearrange page elements to fit your desired format. If you have a definite vision for your site, though, these tools are likely to be inadequate. Google Sites (http://sites.google.com) provides greater control, and the tools on offer are comparable to those of some commercial software packages. Sadly, the interface is a little clunky, and it isn't always easy to achieve the desired results. Paid-for hosting services tend to provide more comprehensive site-building tools, and these sometimes include commercial web-design software.

Whether you opt for an HTML editor or a wizard-based design tool, it's possible to produce an attractive and functional website. Text-based HTML editors give an incredible level of control over the look of your pages and how they function, though it can be hard to focus on design when you're deep in code. Site-builder tools make it easy to focus on the design, but rarely give freedom to produce the site you really want. Our advice is to get to grips with an HTML editor. The time spent learning HTML and CSS at the outset will reap dividends later.

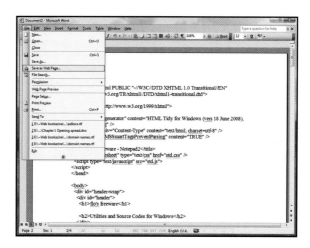

Above: Google Sites allows you to create customised web pages easily, within certain limits

Left: Even Microsoft Word can save documents as web pages

Build a website in 30 minutes

Building a website doesn't have to take weeks. We take you through the process of creating a functioning site using Fasthosts' SiteBuilder

ESSENTIALS ●●●

SKILL LEVEL
Beginner
Intermediate
Expert

HOW LONG
30 minutes

One way of creating a basic but good-looking website is to sign up for a Fasthosts account and use its SiteBuilder tool. We're using the Linux Home hosting package, which costs £3.99 a month; see page 12 for a comparison of packages including this one. It comes with 1.5GB of web space, which may not seem much, but it's more than enough for most people's needs. Most importantly, there's no limit on website traffic (or bandwidth), so you won't incur extra charges or have your website shut down if lots of people visit it.

1 When you sign up, you'll be asked to choose a domain name; the package includes the cost of registering one name. If you already have a domain name, type it into the box and click Next. This will link your existing domain to your Fasthosts package. If you don't already have a domain, enter your desired name and select whether you want the ending to be .com, .co.uk or any of the other 11 options. If the .com name is taken, the next screen will suggest some alternative options you could try.

2 After you've entered your personal and payment details, Fasthosts will send you your username and password. Go to www.fasthosts.co.uk/login and enter these to sign in. You'll then see the Control Panel's Home tab, where you can manage domain registrations, your hosting package, email options and more. Click on the 'You have 1 domain' link. On the next screen, click on the link that appears next to your domain name – for example, it will say Linux Home if you signed up for this package. You'll see an area titled Your website, with links to Easy website creation, Publish your website and three others.

3 Click the SiteBuilder link below Easy website creation. You'll need to activate SiteBuilder and choose a username and password; these don't have to match the login details for your Fasthosts account. You'll then be able to click the link to SiteBuilder. Save this URL as a bookmark so you can return quickly in future. When you subsequently use the link, you must enter your SiteBuilder username and password to log in.

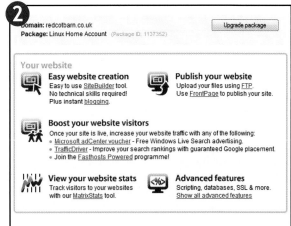

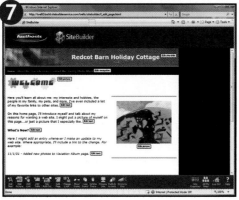

4 You'll see an option to create a new site. Click the Go! button. You're then given the option to start with a multi-page or Express Site template. The latter option lets you answer a few questions to create a single page, with the option to add more pages later. Instead, however, click on the multi-page template link.

5 You can choose from a range of website topics, including Restaurant, Computer Services, Merchant and other options that are probably too specific for your needs. Click the Choose link next to My Personal Site. It doesn't matter which option you choose, as you can customise both the template and the ready-made content later.

6 Type in the name of your website, add a footer if you want one, and tick the pages you want to include from the list. When you click Continue, the SiteBuilder will suggest a template to use for your website; if you don't like it, simply click 'Choose from all designs'. If you click the small paint bucket icon in the bottom right-hand corner of the template, the application will show you which elements in the design you can customise. This usually includes the title colour and image, the main text colour and font, plus the image at the bottom.

7 Once you've chosen a template you like, the application will show you a version of the page filled with default text. This is simply to show you how

your design will look; you can edit virtually every element just by clicking on the yellow Edit button next to it. We've chosen the Abstract Red template, so we can edit the site title, the navigation bar, the pictures and the text. If you want to change to a different template at this point, click the Change Look button in the toolbar at the bottom of the screen. The site title has already been filled in for you, but you can still change it, or change how it looks.

8 We'll start by changing the first paragraph of text. Click the Edit text button and you'll see the edit screen. It's exactly like a word processor; it allows you to make certain words bold, italic or underlined. You can change the colour or font for individual words or even characters if you want. You can even use traditional keyboard short cuts, such as Ctrl-Z to undo any changes you've made. We've enlarged the first character and made it bold.

It's also possible to make numbered lists, indent selected lines and align text left, right or centred. There's a button that lets you link a word or phrase to another web page; we'll come to this shortly. When you've finished editing your text, click Done. You should now see your changes on the web page.

9 Next, change the main picture to something more relevant to your website. Click the Edit picture button, and then 'Choose a different picture'. You haven't uploaded any pictures yet, so click the 'Upload pictures'

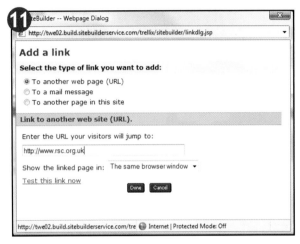

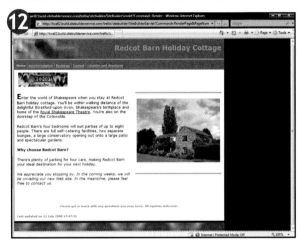

button. You can choose up to 10 pictures at a time. As we're using a Linux-based hosting package, the filenames mustn't have any spaces in them. Click Done and then click the Choose link next to the image you want.

There are several other options to choose from, including image size, alignment, title and caption. Beneath these are useful linking options that enable you to turn the image into a link to a larger version, or a link to another web page. In both cases, you can decide whether to open the image in the same browser window or a new window.

10 When you've edited the text and pictures, you should customise the navigation bar so the text that appears on it is relevant to the pages on your site. Click the 'Edit navigation' button to get to the options. The topmost link doesn't allow you to edit the text, so look further down to the renaming section. Click on each page you want to rename. You can change the Page title for each one, and enter a short version that will appear on the navigation bar. When you have time, you can enter meta tags, which search engines use to rank your website (see page 122 for details).

You can customise the way the navigation bar looks, and even select pictures for each link. Of course, you'll have to create and upload these yourself.

We've opted simply to change the background colour to red and the font colour to silver.

11 The navigation bar allows visitors to jump easily to any page and back again, as it is visible on each page. However, you can also add links to the text itself. We refer to the Royal Shakespeare Theatre on our home page, so it makes sense to link to the theatre's own website. Click the 'Edit text' button next to the paragraph in which you want to make the link. Highlight the words that will form the link in your paragraph and click the 'Make link' button at the top right. Choose 'To another web page (URL)' and then paste the address into the box that appears at the bottom. Click the 'Test this link now' button to make sure the link works (the website will open in a new window) and then click Done.

12 When you've finished editing the text and images on each of the pages you've created, you're ready to make your website live. If you like, you can preview your site beforehand. Once you've checked that everything is to your liking, click the 'Publish to Web' button at the bottom. Immediately, visitors will be able to type your website's address – for example, www.redcotbarn.co.uk – into their browser and visit the site you've just created in 30 minutes.

Web-design software

Whatever your ambitions, there's a web-design program to suit you, from those that build a site to others that let you create dynamic pages

 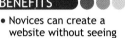
Below: From novices to experts, there's a web-design tool to cater for all skill levels

The internet has been part of our lives for more than 10 years. Time enough, you'd think, for someone to create a web-design package that wasn't frustrating to use. All too often, though, web-design software feels arcane and impenetrable to all but the initiated. We've chosen six programs; some have been designed specifically for beginners, while others are aimed at those with a little more experience.

When you create web pages using HTML and Cascading Style Sheets (CSS), you'll usually start with a blank page, but most web-design software lets you modify a pre-defined template. Alternatively, it may present you with a blank page and some drawing tools for creating a page graphically.

The first thing to consider when choosing a package is the quality of its output. By this we don't just mean whether or not the code conforms to W3C standards

(W3C is the non-profit organisation responsible for web standards). Given that these programs are intended for non-technical users, the quality of the website depends largely on the quality of the templates, its default settings and the advice it provides in its manual or help file.

Some programs have a clumsy or imprecise design environment. Few things are more frustrating, particularly for users who don't want to tweak HTML code. As well as working with HTML, web-design programs should support other web technologies. At the very least, this means being able to create or link to CSS, so that you customise the look of an entire site, applying styles to many pages at once. This is one of the cornerstones of modern web design. You should also look for a program that enables you to use scripting technologies and other dynamic web-design elements. This will mean that you can add photo slideshows, videos, forms and other widgets to your pages.

EASY DOES IT
Ease of use is one of the most important aspects. Key tools and features should be clearly labelled and easy to find, objects on your page should behave logically and predictably and help files should be comprehensive and well written. A good package should also allow you to publish your website to a web server without difficulty.

Even if you consider yourself a novice, you may find that you want to progress beyond the basics later without having to upgrade to a new program. The software should allow you to move from using the visual workspace (usually referred to as the 'what you see is what you get' or WYSIWYG environment) to working directly with the code.

Whether you're artistic and want a blank canvas to work with or you're a geek who loves tinkering, these programs can make web design great fun.

Adobe Dreamweaver CS3

Approximate price: £300 including VAT
Details: www.adobe.com

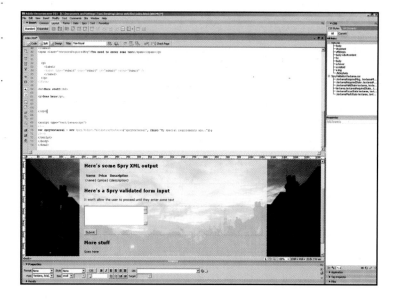

Creative Suite 3 (CS3) is the first version of Dreamweaver to be released since the software passed from Macromedia to Adobe. The price hasn't changed significantly. If you have a copy of Dreamweaver 8, MX 2004 or MX, you can upgrade for around £165 including VAT.

Most of the changes made to the software itself are equally conservative. The main workspace remains largely unchanged from that of Dreamweaver 8. You can use a WYSIWYG design view, a text view for editing source code or a split view that displays both, one above the other. The quality of page rendering in the design view is impressive. It managed to draw one of our test pages, with a CSS-positioned layout and transparent background, more accurately than Internet Explorer 6.

Dreamweaver CS3 supports Adobe's Spry framework. Spry lets you add widgets to your site, as well as transitions that include fades and sliding effects. Some of the transition effects look good if used very sparingly, but the widgets are more useful. These include tools for building accordion page layouts, where clicking on a header causes a related content frame to slide open in the browser, and tabbed panels. If you add Spry elements in design view, Dreamweaver handles the underlying code effortlessly. You can even alter the appearance of Spry elements using CSS.

Dreamweaver CS3 integrates neatly with Photoshop CS3, the Extended version of which is included in the Web Premium package. A new tool called Device Central CS3 allows you to see how your pages will look on mobile devices such as smartphones. It includes emulation for the different versions of Flash Lite used on mobile devices, so it's even more useful if you also use Flash CS3. Adobe Dreamweaver CS3 is an excellent package for more advanced users, but it's expensive.

Namo WebEditor 2006 Suite

Approximate price: £50 including VAT
Details: www.namo.com

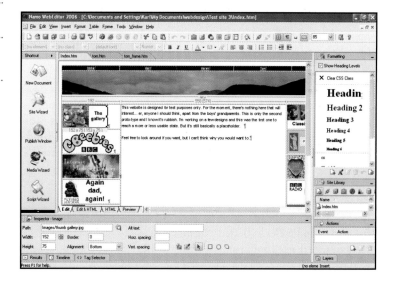

Namo WebEditor has a similar layout to Adobe Dreamweaver (above), with the site library on the left, the Properties Inspector at the bottom of the screen and the main workspace in the centre. Like Dreamweaver, it allows you to work in code, in WYSIWYG mode or in a split screen that shows both. It also puts asterisks next to the names of files that have been modified but not saved. Happily, all this imitation is a good thing: the layout is logical, easy to work with and lets you get a lot done by flicking between the different workspaces.

The property inspector is always visible by default, making the WYSIWYG environment precise and easy to use. Select any element and you can specify most aspects of its appearance and behaviour (colour, alignment on the page or within its container, background colour and so on) by using the Properties Inspector. For fine tweaks, you can switch to working with the underlying code. If you don't want to do this, however, you won't often have to. Jobs such as specifying a page background or linking to an external CSS can be done in the WYSIWYG environment.

Namo WedEditor provides far more hand-holding for novices than Dreamweaver. Using the Media Wizard, for instance, you can embed a music or video file in a web page and specify which program should

play it. You can use the Script Wizard to add dynamic design elements, such as expanding navigation menus and image rollovers, without having to learn a scripting language such as JavaScript (see Chapter 9). There's even a Database Wizard that supports various scripting languages and database connections, so you can create basic database-driven websites. Considering its simplicity, precision and versatility, and its inexpensive price, Namo WebEditor is a great choice.

CoffeeCup HTML Editor 2007

Approximate price: £30 including VAT
Details: www.coffeecup.com

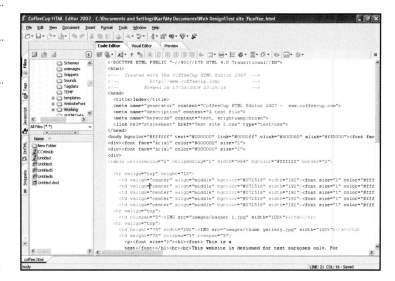

Of all the web design programs here, CoffeeCup HTML Editor 2007 is the one that most requires the user to have some knowledge of HTML. Don't let this put you off, though – there are plenty of reasons to like CoffeeCup, not least its low price.

Originally, CoffeeCup HTML Editor had no WYSIWYG workspace at all, so users had to work with code. Even now, the program's WYSIWYG environment feels underdeveloped compared with those of its competitors. Tasks that you'd normally expect to be able to do with the click of a button, such as specifying a background colour or page transition effect, you will have to do manually by typing the code in the HTML view. However, this isn't as intimidating as it sounds. The program's menus and wizards walk you step by step through fairly complicated tasks, such as creating dynamic HTML elements.

There are a few niggles, however. Having to save the file you're working on each time you switch between code and WYSIWYG editing can become frustrating, and placing images inside a table is also tricky, as they always want to sit on top of the table. Linking to external CSS is easy enough to do in code, but it would be handy to have an automatic tool for this.

Having said that, this is a great editor for anyone who likes to tinker and wants to understand how a website works. If you're prepared to learn HTML, which you can do simply by reading Chapter 3, you can quickly get good results with CoffeeCup HTML Editor. Use the WYSIWYG environment to do the basic formatting, insert text and photos where you want them, and then use the code view to tweak everything into the shape you want. At this price, it's very good value.

Mr Site Takeaway Website

Approximate price: £30 including VAT
Details: www.mrsite.com

Mr Site Takeaway Website is a hosting service that gives you your own .com domain name for a year plus 20 email addresses. We've included it here with the web-design applications because it comes in a box with a complete user manual for the online web-design package. Compared with the web-design tools of other hosting companies, Mr Site's are very good. Designing a simple site takes only a few minutes. Simply choose a template from one of the many on offer, decide on your colour scheme and fill the content frames with text and images. There's a more advanced Creative mode, which lets you add complex formatting and tables to better structure your pages and, if you're feeling particularly confident, start entering the HTML code directly.

The service also allows you to add interactive and dynamic features to your web pages, such as a guestbook and an audio jukebox. As with the basic page elements, you add these features using Mr Site's easy menu system – you don't need to worry about HTML code. You can even include a blog, forum or feedback form, so Mr Site is as sophisticated as it is easy to use. Publishing your site to the web is also easy. Simply click on Publish Your Site and your site becomes live.

Simplicity comes at a price, however. Although there are many templates on offer, they all follow a very similar basic layout: a header, a footer and left-hand navigation. As a result, no matter what stylistic

quirks and odd fonts you apply, your design choices are limited, and the different templates all have a similar look and feel.

This web-design package imposes far more restrictions on your choices than the other packages here. However, when you take into account the speed with which you can get a site online and the fact that the price includes a year's worth of hosting, plus a domain name, Mr Site is good value. It's ideal for anyone who wants to put a good-looking site online quickly without the need for design flair or HTML knowledge.

Serif WebPlus X2

Approximate price: £60 including VAT
Details: www.serif.com

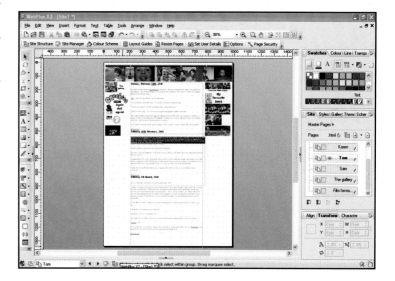

On paper, WebPlus X2 looks a good deal. For just £60 you can design and publish your website, complete with embedded podcasts, RSS feeds, photoblogs and even a convincing online shop.

The 326-page manual is certainly welcome, but it's hardly a sign that the process is going to be straightforward. Even experienced designers will have difficulty getting to grips with the proliferation of menus, tabs and buttons on the screen. Some of the best features, such as the ability to add a podcast or RSS feed, look as if they're going to be easy and then turn out to be anything but. A wizard-based approach to these tasks would have been far better.

WebPlus X2 includes some reasonably attractive templates and the design-oriented interface works rather like a desktop-publishing program, using a combination of drag and drop, dialog boxes and palettes. Again, editing components is sometimes fiddly, especially those found in the ready-made templates. Smart Objects enable you to get forums or blogs up and running in moments. If you don't want to spend time configuring such things, the fact that these are hosted on Serif's own servers will be a blessing.

In fact, WebPlus X2's biggest problem is that its huge array of features and cluttered interface could easily alienate casual users. If this describes you, you're better off with something more limited, such as Mr Site. Another minor reservation is that the program does rather lock you in. The HTML code it generates isn't the worst we've seen, but only the bravest web programmers are likely to want to edit it by hand. If you're prepared to put in some hard work, read the manual and accept that creating a decent website will take more than a few clicks, WebPlus X2 should prove one of the more powerful packages here.

Web.com NetObjects Fusion 11

Approximate price: £150 including VAT
Details: www.netobjects.com

NetObjects Fusion 11 allows even inexperienced users to add dynamic features to their website. The main interface looks a little daunting, but finding what you're looking for is relatively easy.

Fusion helps out as much as it can. When you add an image, it warns you if the graphic is too big and gives you the chance to crop and resize it. When you add a table using the click-and-drag tool, the table fills the area you've created with the cursor, rather than simply using a default cell size. The preview function lets you quickly preview your page in browsers other than Internet Explorer, and you can have multiple pages open in different tabs. The Microsoft Office Ribbon-style bar across the top of the screen also makes it easier to find the tool you're looking for.

New in this version of NetObjects Fusion are Ajax objects. These are dynamic page elements that can be updated from the server independently of the rest of the page's content (this is commonly known as Web 2.0 technology, although this isn't an official standard). There's also a new Timeline feature, similar to Adobe Flash, which gives you more precise control over when objects appear on the page and allows some animation. Both Ajax components and the Timeline are easy to use, if not exactly on the cutting edge of dynamic web content. No programming or design knowledge is required.

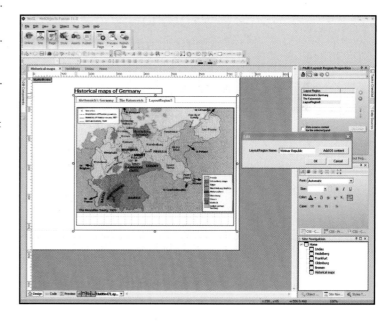

The design approach is template-driven, but most of the designs are cheesy. Access to the underlying code is limited; you can insert and edit your own, but code created by the WYSIWYG editor is locked.

Fusion 11 is more expensive than its competitors, which will rule it out for some users, but if you have an older version of the program, you can upgrade for less than £90.

Planning and designing

Once you've signed up to a hosting package, it's all too easy to plough ahead with your first web page. However, it's essential that you spend some time and effort planning your site. You should pay particular attention to the focus of your website, what to say on each page and how it should look.

Only you can decide on the first two, but entire books are dedicated to the third. In this chapter, we'll show you how to do the groundwork, covering navigation principles, creating a unified look, colour schemes and font choices. You'll also be shown how to make your site accessible to disabled visitors, who may be using software to convert web pages into spoken English. Follow our tips from the start, and you won't have to go back and change code later.

Planning your website

A little time spent on planning your site now will save you hours of frustration later. Follow these easy guidelines for a better-quality site

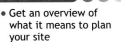

BENEFITS
- Get an overview of what it means to plan your site
- Create a mission statement so have a clear focus for the site

Once you've arranged your hosting package and domain name, it can be tempting to plunge in and design your site as you go, but you'd be asking for trouble. If you attack website development this way, you'll quickly create a sprawling mess of pages, riddled with repetition and annoying navigation quirks – all of which can be avoided with some careful planning.

First, consider the focus of your site. Do you want to sell things to people, or get them to read as many articles as possible? Are you trying to attract advertisers to your site, or simply provide information about a club? You also need to consider your readers. Are they computer-savvy, at home with the latest web technology, or could they be older 'silver surfers' who might be put off by quirky, hard-to-see navigation bars?

Our advice is to start with pen and paper, and write a mission statement for your website. It might sound over the top, but it's worth the effort. Make sure your website is going to give people what they want, whether you're creating a small site for family to keep up to date with a growing baby, or a much bigger site for which you must attract the widest possible audience. If you do want to attract a big audience, aim to give visitors something they can't easily get from another website. There are millions of websites out there; if yours repeats the content of too many others, you'll struggle to get your voice heard above the established players.

MAPPING YOUR WEBSITE

It helps to create a 'map' of your site. Draw a box on the left-hand side of a piece of paper: this is the home page. Decide, in broad strokes, what information will be on it and work your way right. Connect other pages to the home page with lines, and you'll have the beginnings of your navigation structure. At the very least, you'll need an About page or a Contact Us page; these are standard pages that you'll find on virtually every website.

Once you have a list of pages, you'll also have a preliminary version of the file structure of your site. If you're using a control management system (CMS) application such as Joomla (see page 94), this isn't something that you need to worry about. However, if you intend to upload pages manually, you must use a logical folder structure. For instance, you'll need an Images folder for any pictures on your site. It's important that you stick to your own rules; don't store images anywhere else in the name of convenience. Finding files using an FTP client is much harder than it is in Windows, and if you've got random files sprinkled all over your web space, you'll be left with a confusing, unmanageable mess.

KEEPING UP APPEARANCES

Borrowing ideas from your competitors might sound like the fast-track to unoriginality and, worse, potential legal issues. However, one of the best ways to prepare is to spend a few hours online looking for sites you like. Work out what you like about them, and find out if they have anything in common. If they have features you dislike, or if anything slows you down while you're browsing, make a note, and ensure that you don't repeat those mistakes. The most important thing to bear in mind is that the average internet user's attention span is ferociously short. If your site is even remotely frustrating to use, hard to navigate or boring, your visitor will leave and probably never to return. Turn to page 82 if you need a little inspiration on this subject.

At this point, it's worth going back to your notepad and sketching out a few page designs, bearing in mind the traits of your favourite sites. Chances are they'll have a logo in the top-left corner that also acts as a link to take you back to the home page, plus a navigation bar either vertically or horizontally. There may also be a separate list of pages available on the left-hand side. At the very bottom of the page, you might want some small links to your site map, contact pages and other major sections. These are standard design trends and your visitors will expect to find links in these common areas.

HOME IMPROVEMENTS

Assuming first impressions last, you'll want to spend a lot of time on your home page. This is the first thing most visitors will see, unless they're arriving via a Google search that takes them to another page on your site. If your home page doesn't look spectacular, visitors may not get past it. See page 86 for more on graphic design.

Think about the images you can use. You could use a different image every few days to keep things fresh; news sites, in particular, benefit from being constantly updated.

We'll show you how to do this on page 125. You should also think about logos, and whether you want something exciting such as a video (see page 100) on the front page.

CREATION THEORY

Finally, decide how you're going to create your website. Although it's easier to opt for a template-based web-design package, there's more chance of you getting the desired results if you start with a blank canvas and simply use HTML (outlined on page 50) and CSS (see page 64). Using HTML and CSS isn't difficult. Even if you start by using a template from a package such as Namo WebEditor (see page 25), you can take the code it generates and tweak it manually afterwards.

Site for sore eyes Our site plan for Redcot Barn

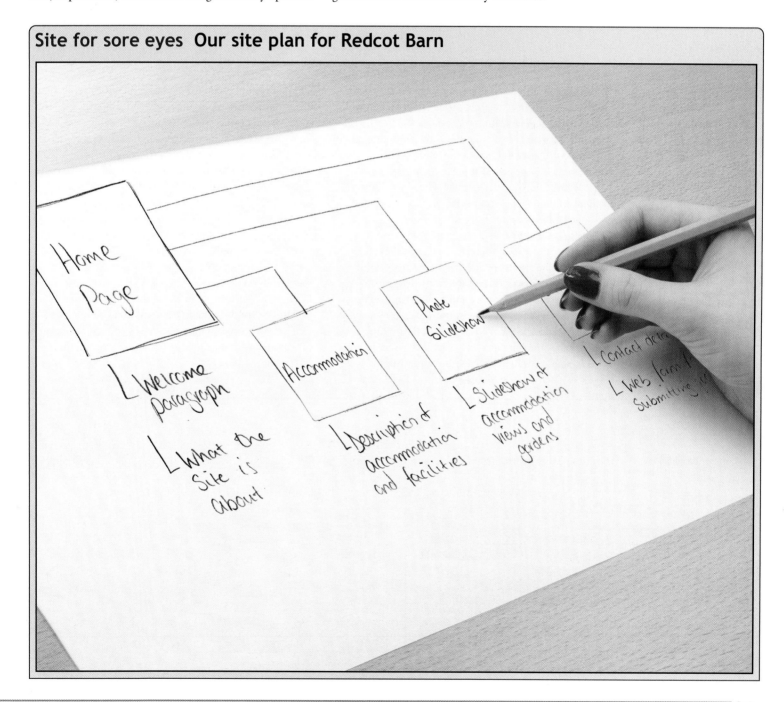

Perfecting your site's navigation

Clear navigation is essential if you want a popular, usable website. Here's how to help your visitors find everything quickly and smoothly

Below left: Wikipedia makes its hyperlinks obvious by using a standard shade of blue

Below right: Amazon's navigation bar on the left-hand side is big, bold, and easy to spot and use

Virtually all websites have a navigational structure, yet it's so easy to get it wrong when making your own site. Navigation is crucial: a frustrated visitor will almost certainly leave and look elsewhere if they can't find what they want on your website. The components of a website that make up its navigation structure are known as navigational elements. These elements should be consistent and easy to understand, and follow internet conventions.

The first thing to consider is your website's name. This isn't normally considered a navigational element, but some visitors will type it to get to your site, and possibly tell others about it as well. For this reason, keep it short and avoid punctuation and unconventional spelling. Keep subfolder names short, too, so users only type www.redcotbarn.co.uk/directions, for example, rather than something unwieldy such as www.redcotbarn.co.uk/resources/widgets/drivingdirections.html.

When people are browsing your site, they're likely to want to return to the home page. This is partly because some visitors will arrive on your site via other pages, thanks to search engine results, and partly because some visitors like to jump back to the home page before using the navigation bar to go to a different page. It's conventional to have a hyperlink to the home page on every single page of your site: this is usually a logo in the top-left corner. It should be the same logo each time and, to avoid confusion, it shouldn't act as a link when the user is already on the home page.

HYPER ACTIVE
Without hyperlinks, or links for short, the internet as we know it simply wouldn't exist. When you're using a web browser, every mouse click takes you to a new page or website. You almost never think about it, and that's how it should be.

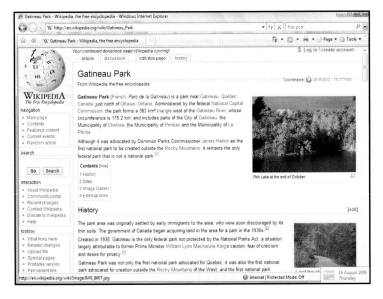

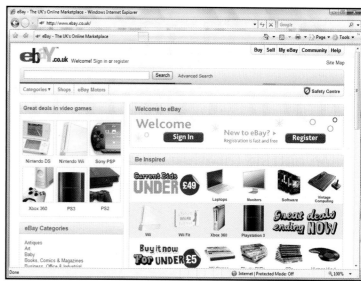

Clicking on a hyperlink is now second nature to almost all internet users. Ask someone to describe a link on a website, and he or she will probably say it's blue, underlined text. Because so many people are familiar with this format, you should think carefully before changing it. If you decide that, for your website to look really great, you simply have to change the appearance of your links, make sure they are distinct from normal text. The easiest way to do this is to make them a different colour, one that really stands out.

If anyone looks at your site and can't immediately tell where all the links are, they won't like it. This becomes even more important if you want people to spend a decent amount of time on your site, reading all that you have to offer. If using the most basic navigational element is too difficult, people won't stay. In his book *Homepage Usability: 50 Websites Deconstructed*, web-usability expert Jakob Nielsen says, "People spend most of their time on other sites than yours". Making your site look distinctive, compared to others, is half the battle. The other half is making sure it still conforms to expected web standards.

The way that links on your site behave is also important. It's usually bad practice to make links open new windows (or tabs) when clicked. Multiple windows are annoying to visitors, who have to wade back through the open windows when they want to return to their first step. However, it's acceptable – if not expected – that links to sites besides your own will open a new tab or window. If you do this, there's a good chance the user will see your site and browse it again when they finish reading the linked-to site and close that window or tab.

RAISING THE BAR
Navigation bars are a common way of getting around a website, and most run horizontally across the top of every page (see page 76). Ideally, navigation bars should be text-based; they're usually narrow, so there isn't room for images. Images can often be mistaken for advertising content, so people are unlikely to click on them.

ON THE BREADCRUMB TRAIL
The term 'breadcrumb trail' has its roots in the fairytale Hansel and Gretel, in which the protagonists ensure they can retrace their steps by leaving a trail of breadcrumbs. A digital breadcrumb trail works in the same way: it is an onscreen representation of every step someone has taken on a website to bring them to their current location. This means that it's possible for them to return to the home page, go back a single step (which the browser's Back button also permits) and, more importantly, go back to any step in between.

So, for example, if a visitor to a website started at the Home page, went to an About page, then on to a Pictures page and then a Holiday page, the breadcrumb trail would look like this:

Home > About > Pictures > Holiday

A breadcrumb trail is hierarchical, and really only works if your website's pages are laid out in a linear way. If your site is a sprawling mass of random pages with no logical path through them, a breadcrumb trail won't add much usability. This gives you another great reason to plan your site carefully and think about the structure of your pages before you start uploading anything.

AND FINALLY...
Perhaps the most important thing to remember when designing your site's navigation is to keep it simple. Animated, drop-down navigation bars and breadcrumb trails are navigational niceties, and there's certainly room for them. But if your site is illogically laid out or flouts navigational norms, these tools will add nothing.

Above left: The First Post doesn't have a breadcrumb trail but it uses a standard three-column layout

Above right: eBay uses a navigation bar and a breadcrumb trail so users can retrace their steps

Limiting your content

When putting together your website, remember that less is more. By limiting the look and feel, you are actually maximising its impact

- Keep the content on your site focused, concise and relevant
- Use language your target audience will understand

The internet is full of billions of pages, all bursting with information, which means you're going to have to offer something unique if you want to be noticed. The temptation here is to try to offer everything under the sun to become a one-stop hit for people, so they can get all they want on one site.

This will inevitably lead to a website that is a jack of all trades and master of none. You should stick to your area or areas of expertise, so people can trust what they read. If your aim is to create a website about spiders in the UK yet you know little about the subject, you're setting yourself up for failure. Anyone who visits your site and knows more than you, or has read conflicting information on another website that they trust, will immediately take a dislike to your site and never return.

It's best to limit your content and please a smaller group of people who visit your site, rather than offering a diluted experience for the masses that will leave them dissatisfied. If you believe that another website is already the best in the business at something, you mustn't settle for trying to produce a similar, but inferior, offering that will only look bad by comparison.

LIMITING DESIGN

Your website's design should help people to find what they want. This has two main components. First, you need to make sure that you use one design for your site, so people don't become confused when attempting to navigate your pages. It will help to give your whole site a unified look, something we touch upon in more detail on page 36. Second, you need to keep your pages short. Enormous pages that run to thousands of words and contain dozens of images will make it hard for readers to locate the information that's relevant to them. Such

TIP
Focus on what you know and keep all the content on your site relevant. When planning your site, nail down its remit, stick to it, and avoid irrelevant tangents.

Right: Craigslist has one of the most understated front pages on the internet. Where other sites use images or icons, Craigslist limits itself to the most relevant content

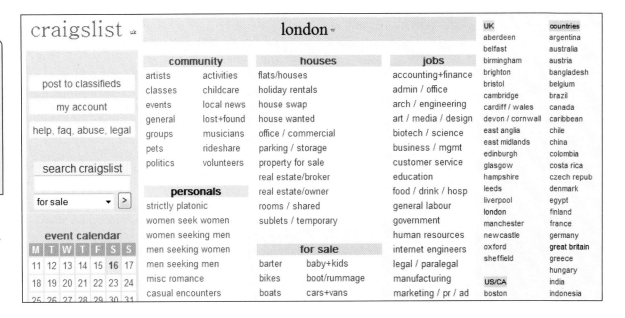

pages also take a long time to load, which is annoying for those with slow internet connections.

Keep vertical scrolling to a minimum. People who own a desktop computer are likely to have a mouse with a scroll wheel, so will have some tolerance for scrolling down web pages. However, laptop users don't have such easy methods for scrolling, and will quickly get frustrated. The one exception to this rule is blogging, where users expect posts to be stored in a long list. Even here, regular readers won't need to scroll, as they'll probably read only the first post, which should be at the top of the page.

What you absolutely must avoid is a design that forces your visitors to scroll horizontally. It's impossible to build a website that takes account of every conceivable resolution, especially when this can include mobile devices such as smartphones. However, you should aim to make a website that requires no horizontal scrolling for people who are running their monitors at 1,024x768. Keeping your design narrow is also a good idea; it's easier for your eye to scan back across a narrow column of text than it is a wider one.

LIMITING PAGES

When we say that you should limit your pages, we don't mean that you should pare down your plan and have only four or five pages. But you need an appropriate number of pages for the amount of content you wish to present.

If you find that your pages routinely run to thousands of words, it's worth considering how to cut things down to a more reasonable level. This will often mean creating another page, which is linked to with a Next button.

On the other hand, if you find that some of your planned pages have only a few dozen words on them, there will be an awful lot of empty space. You should combine these small pages into one larger page, and then split that into sections. Perhaps the only thing readers hate more than having to scan thousands of words on one page is constantly having to click to a new page, because there are only a few words on each one.

LIMITING LANGUAGE

We've talked about working out who your audience will be, but you should also consider the language they will understand. If you want scientists to visit your site and do business with you, opt for a conservative style. If you want young people to visit, you can be more relaxed and informal, but beware of language that could be perceived as patronising or vague. Confused readers probably won't take the time to ask you to explain yourself.

People tend to spend only a few seconds on each page until they find what they're looking for, and only then will they take the time to read thoroughly, so cut out the waffle and stick to the point. On page 39, we'll take a closer look at the language you should use on your site.

Above left: Wired.com's front page is extremely long, but the main stories and points of interest are right at the top

Above middle: The New York Times' front page is difficult to use due to the sheer number of boxes, columns and sidebars

Above right: Conversely, the BBC's news page is relatively short. It's customisable and each section can be shown or hidden to keep things neater

Creating a unified look

To make life as easy as possible for your visitors, you should apply the same design elements, colours and fonts throughout your website

BENEFITS ●●●●

- Consistent page design and a familiar look that will help your visitors navigate your site
- Learn which colours and fonts work best

We have already seen that if the navigational elements on a website are all over the place, and the link that takes visitors back to the homepage is constantly moving and changing size, then navigating your site will become a chore and, ultimately, it will cost you readers.

Approach the visual style in exactly the way we suggested on page 34 and follow the maxim of less is more. The best way to bring a unified look to your website is to use CSS; this will be covered in detail in Chapter 4. CSS ensures that elements on your site have exactly the same look throughout. If you change a design

Right: It's easy to see the consistent look across these four pages of our website

  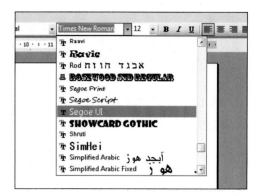

element or a font in CSS, every instance of that element or font will change across your entire site.

IT'S HUE YOU KNOW

Choosing your website's colour scheme can be tricky. Using a few colours on a website can be effective, as it will emphasise certain parts of your site and draw attention to different elements. However, you need to think like a professional designer and become familiar with the concept of complementary colours: these are pairs of colours that are opposite each other on the colour wheel, such as blue and orange, for example. Two such colours provide harmonious contrast.

Along with this, it's worth bearing in mind that shades of the same colour – such as the shades of green that we've used on our Redcot Barn website – can help to create a sense of consistency and familiarity.

Rather than trying to pick colours manually, we recommend Adobe's Kuler (http://kuler.adobe.com). We've included an in-depth guide on how to use this tool on the next page. Kuler will pick five colours according to the rules you select, and you can then copy their hexadecimal (Hex) values, which are shown underneath them. You'll need these, since HTML and CSS both use Hex values for defining colours.

WHAT'S YOUR TYPE?

Think carefully about your choice of font. The rule that applies to printed material such as this book applies on websites, too: don't use more fonts than you need. In fact, you should try to limit your choice to two fonts, and use only these throughout your site.

It's true that there are some striking-looking typefaces out there, but unless you're using your website to make a specific statement about design, you should stick to the classics. Times New Roman is a safe, easy-to-read font that works in most web browsers, while Georgia is a good alternative when it comes to serif fonts (the typeface you're reading now is a serif font). Sans serif fonts – such as those used for the title and standfirst on the opposite page – should be used as your second font. Arial or Tahoma are good choices. It's really up to you to decide whether you choose serif or sans serif for the titles

and heading; just make sure that you use the other type for the body copy.

Consistency is as important as the fonts that you finally settle on. You need to make sure that the font you use is not only the same throughout your site, but also the same size, and you must use styles such as bold and italics consistently.

Even humble links needs thinking about. There are various ways of styling a link, such as underlined, underlined only when you hover the mouse over it and so on. However, the web standard is to underline the link and colour it in a standard shade of blue. Whatever you choose to do, avoid making your links blend into the page. If people can't instantly identify a link, they won't know to click it.

SNAP DECISIONS

To maintain your unified look, try to make sure that any images you use appear in roughly the same places on each page. An image-editing program such as Adobe Photoshop Elements will allow you to change the dimensions of an image before you upload it. This is doubly important for pages that contain multiple images.

Furthermore, text should flow around the images in the same way throughout your website. If the pictures have captions, those captions should have the same font at the same size.

IS IT COMPATIBLE?

There's no point having a consistently applied design if it doesn't display properly in certain browsers. Different browsers support different web standards, which is something you'll need to bear in mind if you have hopes of reaching a wide audience. To find out about testing the compatibility of your website without having to install every version of every browser, see page 49.

You'll also need to think about the resolution of your site. You might have a 24in monitor with a resolution of 1,920x1,200, but few of your potential visitors will. If you design your site to a width of 1,920 pixels, most people will quickly leave it. Instead, work to a width of 1,024 pixels, which should make your site compatible with just about everyone's monitor.

Above left: Apple's website is an excellent example of unified design. New visitors should be able to navigate with ease

Above middle: Auction giant eBay might be great for bagging a bargain, but its design isn't the best, particularly because it uses lots of different fonts

Above right: Your computer may have hundreds of fonts installed, but you should stick to using just two of them

Using Adobe Kuler

If you want to select a colour scheme for your site and you're stuck for ideas, look no further than Adobe's free Kuler service

K uler (pronounced 'colour') is a useful online application designed to help you select the appropriate colour scheme for your website. There are thousands of pre-made colour schemes to choose from, and you can also create your own. Here we'll explain how Kuler works.

WHEEL OF FORTUNE

Go to http://kuler.adobe.com and click on the 'Create link' on the left-hand side. You'll see a colour wheel at the top and a set of five points within it. One has a white circle around it; this is the base colour. Drag this point to the colour you want, and the other four will follow it to create a scheme. By default, the Analogous rule is selected, which means the four secondary colours are similar to the base colour. You can change this – at the left of the colour wheel – to six other presets, including Complementary, Monochromatic and Custom. You can also drag one of the four secondary points to a colour of your choice, and the remaining three will automatically move to other colours that match the chosen rule.

Below each of the five colour swatches shown, you'll see sliders and values where you can adjust the colour. It's worth noting these values down. Here, the relevant value is in the Hex box; right-click on each box to copy its value.

PIC 'N' MIX

If you want the colour scheme to match a photo, click the From an Image option below the Create heading. Below the photo that appears are two buttons: Upload and Flickr. Click Upload and browse to the image you want to use. Once it's uploaded, a scheme is chosen based on the Mood menu. Choose from Colorful, Bright, Muted, Deep, Dark or Custom. If you move any of the circles, the scheme changes to a Custom colour scheme, where circles can be moved independently of each other.

Unless you register for an account, you can't save your scheme and you can't get the Hex values. However, if you have an image editor with a colour picker that shows the Hex values, you could take a screenshot of the scheme and then hover the picker over each colour in the screenshot to see its values.

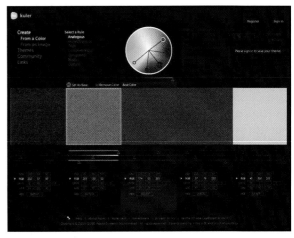

Left: Create a colour scheme by uploading a photo. Kuler will automatically select colours from it according to the rule you choose

Right: Colour schemes can also be created using a standard colour wheel

Writing for the web

Make sure the language you use on your website is presentable and holds the reader's attention by checking spelling, grammar, phrasing and tone

It sounds obvious to say you should make sure there are no spelling mistakes or grammatical errors in your website, but it's often overlooked in the excitement of finishing your design. Sadly, nothing makes a site look amateurish quite like sloppy editing and bad spelling.

You should type the words that will appear on your site into a word processor such as Microsoft Word or the free OpenOffice.org Writer, and run the spellchecker and grammar checker before you publish. Reading material onscreen is harder to follow than on paper, so don't make life even harder for your readers by forcing them to read confusing sentences littered with spelling mistakes, poor grammar and improper punctuation.

Then take a few tips from the professionals. Every magazine and newspaper has a style guide, a document in which troublesome words are listed and their correct spelling and use set in stone. This enables you to spell words consistently and also helps in situations when several people contribute to a site. Making sure the quality of your language is of a high standard will make your site easier to read.

There is another very good reason to keep an eye on your spelling. People searching on Google and other search engines will generally use the correct spelling of technical terms when searching. Even if they don't, most search engines will detect a spelling mistake and suggest a correction. If you've misspelled any keywords, your site is less likely to be found by the people searching for them.

A QUICK WORD

Not only do people find it harder to read from a screen than they do from paper, but they also have a much shorter attention span when reading websites. A study carried out in 2005 by students at the universities of Hamburg and Hannover suggested that web users look at each page for an average of 12.5 seconds, which isn't much time to get your point across.

It has also been suggested that internet users don't read a web page in the same way they would, say, the front page of the *Sunday Times*. People skim a web page briefly, hunting for key words or phrases. If your site has lots of filler paragraphs or extra words, casual users will leave very quickly. To keep people's attention, you need to make sure there's a pay-off in every paragraph you write, something that provides the information they want.

●●●● BENEFITS
- Make your website look professional by eliminating typos and bad grammar
- Keep visitors interested by writing concisely

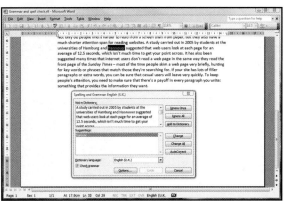

Top left: If you don't spell keywords correctly, your site won't appear in Google when people search for those terms

Bottom left: Word processors have built-in spelling and grammar checkers, so use them

Making your website accessible

When designing your website, you should consider the needs of disabled visitors, particularly those who are blind or partially sighted

BENEFITS ●●●

- Ensure that all visitors can access the content on your site
- Avoid the possibility of legal action being taken by disabled users who cannot access content

Below left: How the Pizza Hut website looks to someone who has Protanopia (red-green colour blindness)

Below right: How the website looks to someone with normal sight

W e've already talked about the importance of keeping your website focused, both in terms of its content and its design, but there's another crucial aspect you need to consider: accessibility. Some of the people who visit your site will be using different monitors to yours, running at different resolutions. More importantly, some users will have poor eyesight, or could be blind. How do you make sure that your website is user-friendly to people with these limitations?

To ensure that you don't alienate this group of users, you might need to make some changes to the way you code your site. There is a chance that, as they browse your site, these users will be using a screen reader, which reads the words out loud. Some screen readers are more advanced than others, but in all cases you can help direct people in the right direction. If you stick to the guidelines outlined here, and remember to use clean HTML and CSS (as outlined in Chapters 3 and 4), it shouldn't be hard to make your website more accessible.

ACCESS ALL AREAS

One of the most important elements in web design, as we discussed on page 32, is well thought-out, user-friendly navigation. However, navigation is more challenging for users with disabilities. If you use JavaScript or Flash for your navigation bar, screen readers may not be able to interpret the links. An easy alternative is to use CSS.

Users will often want to increase the font size or remove the images to make web pages easier to read. If you use images for the buttons of your navigation bar, any text embedded within them cannot be 'seen' by the screen readers, so your site will be impossible to navigate. However, as long as images aren't the fundamental part of your site's navigation, you should be OK.

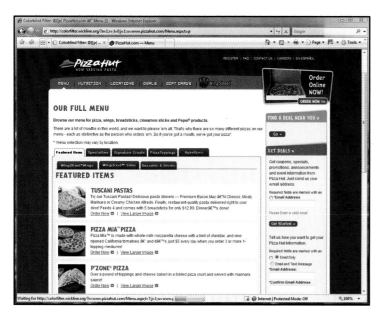

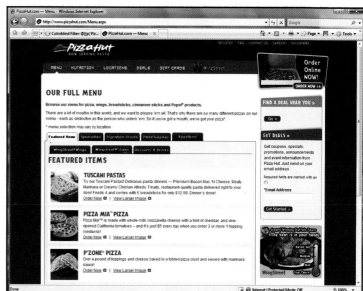

Another easy way to help people is to use the `<alt>` tag for every image. Including a simple description such as `<img alt="Photo of the garden"` means that a screen reader can describe the image to a user with disabilities. Also, if a visitor chooses to turn off the images on your site, they're left with the `<alt>` tags and the main words on the page. If you don't enter an `<alt>` tag, any visitor turning off the images won't benefit from a description of what should be there.

Another point relates to layout. Be careful using tables to construct the layout of web pages, as even the smartest screen reader software can struggle to understand them. However, tables can be made accessible. If you use one, keep it simple and avoid empty table cells. An able-bodied visitor may take only a few seconds to process the information in a table, but someone with impaired sight has to wait while their screen reader reads every cell.

MISSING LINKS

Provide users with keyboard short cuts to navigate your site by including the accesskey attribute in your links. For example, `<a href="../contact.html" accesskey="C">` lets the user press Alt or Ctrl plus C to follow the link. It's best not to use Accesskeys for all links, but it's useful for the main navigation bar. The most popular screen reader, JAWS, can read Accesskeys aloud, allowing users to access pages more quickly.

You should also add the `<title>` attribute in links. This gives visitors clearer guidance on where the link will take them. For example, a link named 'au/index.html' won't help anyone, but if you add the title `attribute title="Opens the about us page"` it will be much clearer to anyone listening to a screen reader.

Using the right colours for important navigation elements such as links is particularly important for users who are colour-blind. Tools such as http://colorfilter. wickline.org will simulate how pages appear to colour-blind users. If you make a quick check that your chosen colour doesn't disguise a link as normal text, your site will be accessible to the widest possible number of users.

There are several tools that will check your HTML to make sure that it adheres to the Web Accessibility Initiative (WAI) accessibility guidelines; a good example can be found at www.etre.com/tools/accessibilitycheck. You can also download a free web-accessibility toolbar from www.visionaustralia.org.au/ais/toolbar. This simulates the experiences of different types of user, and also provides links to other accessibility resources.

KEEP IT LEGAL

If you don't take steps to make your site readable by those with disabilities, be warned: there are legal implications. The Disability Discrimination Act (DDA) states, "If you haven't made reasonable adjustments to make your website accessible then you may be liable under the Act". It's your responsibility to ensure that

Is your site accessible?

The best way of checking that your website is accessible is to strip away some of the elements in your site. In Internet Explorer, go to the View menu. Under Text Size, select Largest. Test to see if your navigation bar is still working.

If it is, open Internet Explorer's Internet Options under the Tools menu. Click the Accessibility button under the General tab. Take away a few formatting options and see what your site looks like now. You should see only the bare bones of your site. It may look dull, but if the navigation still works well, your site is already significantly better than one with poor navigation.

Below: How the BBC website looks with the text larger and CSS turned off

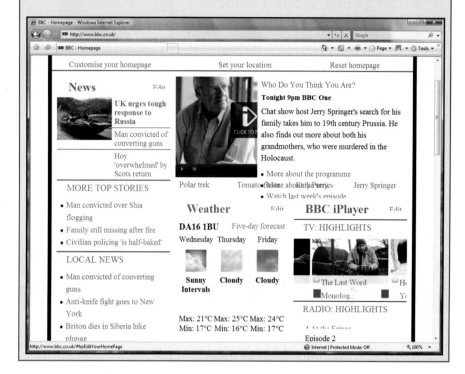

your website doesn't discriminate against disabled visitors. A disabled person can make a claim against you and your website if it's impossible or unreasonably difficult to access information and services.

It really isn't difficult to make 'reasonable adjustments' to your site. You just have to make sure that your website meets Word Wide Web Consortium (W3C) standards for good website design. This means passing Priority 1 Web Content Accessibility Guidelines with valid HTML and CSS. For details of what this entails, you should visit www.w3.org/tr/wcag10. If you follow all the guides mentioned there, your site will pass Priority 1 with ease.

If you already have a website and don't want to make fundamental changes to it, there are provisions under the act for you to create a separate version of your site which is accessible, but only "if all else fails".

Redcotbarn.co.uk

You've bought the book, now visit the website! See the techniques we've used in action, and download our example files for your own use

Our banner shows a random photo each time the page is viewed. Learn how to do it on pages 125-127.

Images are a fundamental part of virtually every website. On pages 54-55 and 84-85 we show you how to optimise and place them.

Links are another integral part of every site. On pages 56-57 you can find out how to add links and style them to your liking.

Creating borders around CSS layers is simple, and you don't need to have plain lines. Turn to page 67 to find out more.

Luxury holiday cottage in S

Enter the world of Shakespe
Situated in a quiet location s
drive from the delightful Str
your ideal choice for accomr
Shakespeare's birthplace.

This historic area has many
that will appeal to all ages a
Shakespeare Theatre, Mary
cottage, which are only a sh
Blenheim Palace, Ragley Ha
properties are close by - inc
Gardens. Or, you can simply
countryside. You're also on t
its picturesque villages and
break from work.

Redcot Barn's four bedroom:
people. There are full self-c
lounges, a large conservator
spectacular gardens. There's
cars, and pets are welcome.
atmosphere, you will be ass

Accomodation | Tariffs | Gallery | Di

re country

you stay at Redcot Barn.
d by fields, yet only a short
on-Avon, Redcot Barn is
f you want to explore

s. There are places to visit
, including the Royal
ouse and Anne Hathaway's
away. Warwick Castle,
herous National Trust
world famous Hidcote
e beautiful Warwickshire
ep of the Cotswolds, with
s - ideal for a relaxing

parties of up to eight
cilities, two separate
out onto a large patio and
parking for up to four
with a friendly
axing and pleasurable stay.

Current Temperature
Stratford-Upon-Avon

Today
15°C
Partly Cloudy

Friday
16°C

Saturday
16°C

❝ Redcot Barn is
your ideal choice for
accommodation if you
want to explore
Shakespeare's
birthplace ❞

We've used images for
the backgrounds of our
navigation bar buttons to
create a 'tabbed' look. See
pages 76-79 for details.

Round corners can provide
a break from square ones.
We'll show you various ways
to make round corners on
pages 134-136.

Adding gadgets such as a
weather forecast is really
easy. Find out how to add
this and many other exciting
widgets in Chapter 7.

Pullquotes can be useful to
draw readers into a page.
They're easy to add using the
CSS we show you on page 67.

ut Us | Advanced Projects | Site Map

Anatomy of a web page

If you want to build the best website possible, you need to understand the HTML code web browsers use to display web pages. It sounds daunting, but HTML is written in plain English and is actually easy to learn.

In this chapter, you'll learn everything you need to know about HTML tags. We'll explain how to use these tags to create a web page by formatting text, including images, creating lists and tables, and adding links. Whether you plan to create all your pages from scratch in HTML or use an HTML editor, it's vital that you are able to edit and fine-tune the code to get your pages looking exactly the way you want them.

You'll also learn how to make your pages work in different web browsers, and how to upload your finished pages to your web space.

How to begin

You may be itching to start your first web page, but first you need to be familiar with all the various page elements and how to manage them

BENEFITS ●●●
- Understand folder structure and how your site should be broken up
- Learn about web browsers and how to make sure your website works with them all

Below: These two pages are different, but appear to have the same filename. This is because filenames are case-sensitive

One of the real secrets to effective web design is careful planning and organisation. This works on two levels. First, you need to ensure that your site is focused, well laid out and easy to navigate, as we explained in the last chapter. Second, you should manage it in such a way that it is easy to find your way around and locate those pages that require a tweak, an update or a wholesale revamp.

GETTING ORGANISED

Before you do anything else, then, you should create a folder on your computer that will store your site, and make sure that you only ever work in this directory. It's tempting to put this on the desktop to make it easy to find, but this is rarely a good way to work. Using the desktop as anything other than a temporary resting place

for files in transit is a sure-fire way to clutter things up, and it will lead to the kind of situation that ultimately slows you down.

Instead, head for your My Documents folder and create a new folder. Over the next few chapters, we'll be developing a basic website to demonstrate how the whole process works. Our site is devoted to a ficticious holiday cottage called Redcot Barn, so we'll simply call our folder Redcot Barn. Inside it, we'll create another folder called 'images' where we'll store all the graphics, and additional folders for each major section of the site.

Careful planning here will make all the difference when you put your site online. Organising all your images in one place makes them easy to find when you want to re-use them on more than one page, and creating new folders for every section will help you to keep your

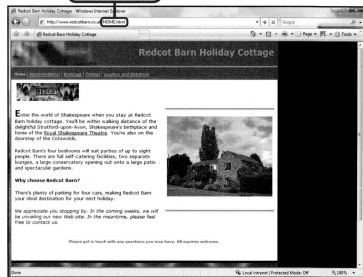

page addresses short and easy to remember. It might even improve your chances of coming out top in a Google search.

CASE SENSITIVITY

Windows doesn't make any distinction between upper- and lower-case characters, but many web servers do. The most common web server operating system is Linux, which, having its roots in Unix, sees no greater similarity between 'a' and 'A' than it does between 'X' and 'Y'.

This only holds true for the filename of a web page, not the domain name. While WWW. REDCOTBARN.CO.UK and www.redcotbarn.co.uk would both get you to the same place, you could conceivably store three different pages at www. redcotbarn.co.uk/HOME.html, www.redcotbarn.co.uk/ home.html and www.redcotbarn.co.uk/Home.html. There are times when this could be useful but, generally speaking, using anything other than lower-case characters introduces an extra level of complexity to your address. It means you have to spell out every part in detail and rely on your visitor to type it in exactly. By sticking with lower-case throughout, you can tell people verbally to go to 'red cot barn dot co dot uk slash home dot html', rather than 'red cot barn dot co dot uk slash capital h, lower-case o-m-e, dot lower-case h-t-m-l'.

Any page whose filename can be put directly after your domain, such as the home.html in the example above, appears directly inside the folder you created on your hard disk and not in any subfolders held within it. When you transfer it to your domain – that is, your online web space – it will also appear in the top level there, This, conversely, is called the 'root'. We will use this naming convention throughout this section.

USING FOLDERS ONLINE

As your site grows, organisation becomes ever more important, and subdirectories become key to effective organisation. These form the words between the slashes on your site. So, if we wanted to create a series of local information pages for our holiday home business's website, we could create /cotswolds-attractions.html, /stratford-attractions.html and /london-attractions.html, but this would add three more pages to the root directory of our website. This can get confusing and cluttered, just as your Windows desktop does when you drop files there.

It is better to create a separate folder into which you can save all pages with a similar theme. In our example, then, we would create a folder called /attractions/ into which we would save three pages: cotswolds.html, stratford.html and london.html.

The other advantage of creating folders is that you can create extremely logical filenames that get your readers to your pages more quickly and with less effort. You cannot rely on repeat visitors to remember the exact filename of every page on your site. There's a chance

they'll try /attractions/cotswolds.htm, cotswolds.shtm and cotswolds.php, before giving up and looking elsewhere for the information they need.

Creating a new folder inside /attractions/ called cotswolds, and saving the Cotswolds page inside this folder using the name index.html, means it will load automatically whenever someone visits redcotbarn.co.uk/ attractions/cotswolds. You can see for yourself how much easier this is to remember than the cumbersome redcotbarn.co.uk/attractions/cotswolds.html.

CHOOSING THE RIGHT FILENAMES

Carefully thought-out and logically named folders and pages don't only help your readers, but they also help Google. Optimising your directory and filenames in this way and giving them addresses that relate to their contents ensures that they are indexed more effectively, increasing your chances of showing up on the first page of any set of search results. For a business, this means increased traffic and the potential for a commensurate boost in income. For more information on how to make your site Google-friendly, you should follow the project on page 122.

You should use a small number of hyphens to break your page addresses into logical sections, so folders are called brewing-winemaking, local-transport and walking-tours rather than 'brewing and winemaking', 'local transport' and 'walking tours'.

Although web browsers can now handle character spaces, the result in the browser's address bar is ugly, as each space is replaced by '%20'. Potentially, this will render a site about the Twenty 20 cricket league as Twenty%2020.htm and can introduce untold confusion. Other characters outside of a specific subset are likewise swapped out for their ASCII code equivalents.

Above: When you're creating your website, you should store the pages on a local hard disk and not on your web space

Knowing the rules will help you. Internet regulation RFC 1734 specifies how addresses should be encoded when used in a browser. It permits the numbers 0 to 9, the letters a to z in their lower- and upper-case variations, and the characters $-_.,+!*'(and). This gives plenty of scope for creating unique and memorable addresses for every page on your site, with dashes, underscores or dots used in place of spaces. However, we recommend that you avoid $!*'(and) because they are confusing to spell out when you read an address aloud; $ could be called string or dollar, while (and) aren't actually brackets (which are [and]) but parentheses. Incidentally, { and } are braces and as they render as %7B and %7D, they should also be avoided in any page or folder names.

MAPPING THINGS OUT

You may find it helps to draw out a sketch of the directory structure of your proposed site at this stage, and use this as a map for when it comes to building the pages. This will help you to ensure that you have included all relevant information and linked all your pages appropriately. In particular, it will show you the relationship between related pages gathered together in a folder, so you can link cotswolds.html, stratford.html and london.html both to each other and to the top-level /attractions/ folder, in which you should create an introductory page called index.html; this will introduce the local area in broad strokes, before presenting a menu of links to the pages mentioned above for a more detailed exploration of each area.

Work logically through this map, starting with your homepage, which should appear at the top of a tree, whose branches fan out like a family tree. Ensure that there is an easy way back to the top of the structure for anyone who needs to return to your homepage (most commonly implemented through a logo, graphic or text link, such as Home, in the top-left of the page) and resist the temptation to publish any pages that are incomplete.

Below: Use services such as Browsershots to preview how images will look in different browsers without having to install them on your system

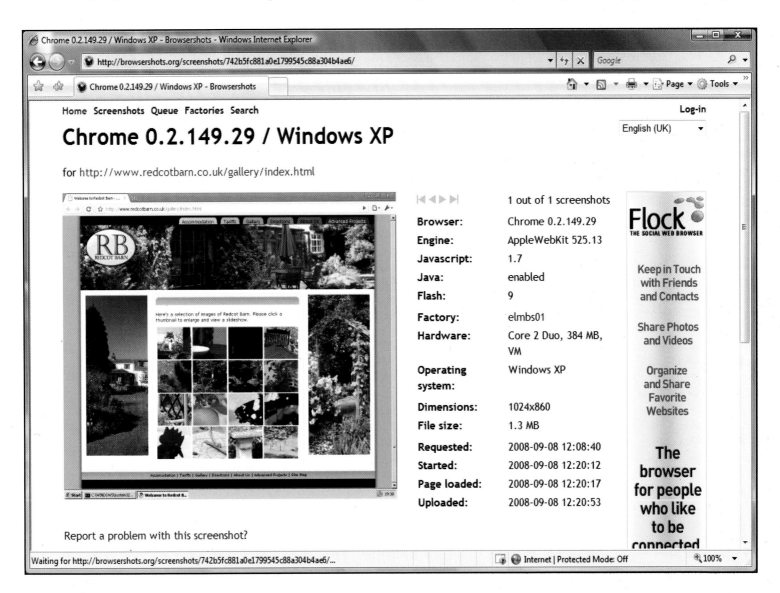

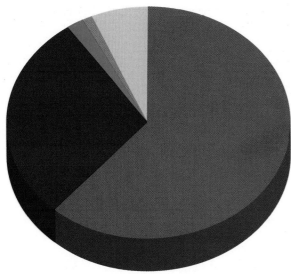

- ● Internet Explorer (61.4%)   ● Opera (1.1%)
- ● Firefox (29%)   ● Other browsers (6.5%)
- ● Safari (2%)

Five steps to methodical web design

1 Gather together related pages in parent folders that allow your readers to type the shortest possible web address every time. This makes them easier to remember, and easier to pass on by word of mouth.

2 Use logical file and folder names to give yourself the best chance of coming top in search engine results lists.

3 Avoid obscure characters in file and folder names, and use logical punctuation such as dashes, underscores and dots rather than spaces.

4 Test, test and re-test your pages at every stage of construction. Don't be tempted to cater only for Internet Explorer or screen sizes above 1,024x768 pixels, or you risk losing a sizable chunk of your potential audience.

5 Never publish your pages until they are complete and ready for public consumption. Pages that are still 'under construction' look unprofessional, and may even discourage visitors from returning to your site.

UNDER CONSTRUCTION

Even if you mark pages as works in progress, it looks unprofessional and is guaranteed to have your visitors heading straight back to Google for alternatives.

TESTING, TESTING

You should test your site at every stage of production. As you may include many common elements on every page, you should not leave testing until the end (or ignore it altogether), as any problems you find could affect every page on your site. It's far better to test as you go, and tackle problems as and when they arise.

Don't be tempted to assume that everyone uses the same browser as you. Most visitors to your site will use Internet Explorer (see the pie chart above), but its market share is being eroded with the growth of serious competitors. W3Counter (www.w3counter.com) puts Internet Explorer's combined market share at 61.4 per cent, Firefox versions 1 to 3 at 29 per cent, Safari at two per cent and Opera at 1.1 per cent. Other browsers, including Google's new Chrome, make up the remaining six-and-a-half per cent. To put this in perspective, over eight million people in 25 countries downloaded Firefox 3 in the 24 hours after its official release. If you only test your site with IE7, thereby disregarding the significant number of people using alternative browsers to Internet Explorer, you'll be doing your site a massive disservice.

You don't have to install every possible browser on your PC to test your pages. Just upload them to a development directory on your web server and use a service such as Browsershots (http://browsershots.org) to test pages on your behalf. Tell it where the pages can be found and which pages you'd like it to use in the test, and it will visit them in each browser and present you with a

screenshot of the results in Windows, Linux and Mac OS X, so you can check if there are any problems, or if certain elements are displayed differently.

REMEMBER...

If you're still in the process of developing pages, do not link the development folder to the root of your web space, where they will be easy to find and confuse with a finished site. Develop everything on your hard disk, and upload pages to the web space only when you need to test them or when they're ready for public consumption.

Pages will work in almost the exact same way on a hard disk as they would when published on the internet. Double-clicking a page on your drive will open it in your browser; clicking any links that it contains will take you to the pages to which they refer.

You're bound to spend many hours developing your site, so it makes sense to create a backup of the folder you've created in your My Documents folder. You shouldn't need to buy an expensive external hard disk for this, since your site is unlikely to occupy more than a couple of gigabytes. A low-capacity USB flash drive should suffice; even 4GB models cost as little as £10.

Top left: Internet Explorer is by far the most widely used web browser. However, you should test that your website appears correctly on other browsers, too

Basic HTML tags

Even a basic understanding of the way HTML tags work will help enhance the way your web pages look and make them more appealing to visitors

A web page can be as simple or complex as you want it to be. Typing the word 'hello' into a file called index.htm, saving that to your computer's hard disk and then opening it in your browser will display the simplest yet least engaging web page you could ever hope to encounter. However, by surrounding your content with tags that describe what it is and how it should look, you can produce something that will be more pleasant to read and is likely to hold your visitors' attention for much longer.

HAPPY COUPLES

Web pages are programmed in plain English. Because many tags use words that could also be used in your content – such as 'head', 'body' and 'align' – they are always encased in angled brackets. Tags are used in pairs, where one half of the pair switches on an effect or opens a particular section, such as a paragraph, and the other half of the pair, which uses the same tag name preceded by a forward slash (/), switches it off.

For example, the line of HTML that is shown in Figure 1 would be rendered as shown in Figure 2. This is a paragraph using bold, bold italic, plain italic and underlined text.

Notice how the bold italic text is rendered that way because the bold tag <b> was already in use when we applied the italic tag <i>. We also switched off the italic tag </i> before switching off the bold tag </b>, and then opened the italic tag again for the words 'plain italic'. We could have left the italic tag open throughout and just closed off the bold tag after the words 'bold italic', but it's good practice not to have your tags overlapping. Any tag that opens within another tag should be closed off before you close the container tag. You can re-open it again immediately outside of that container if necessary.

The tag <u>, which we used to underline our text, is no longer widely used, and you should avoid underlining text because it makes the words look like a link to another page. For emphasis, you can make text

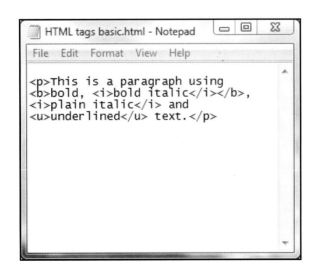

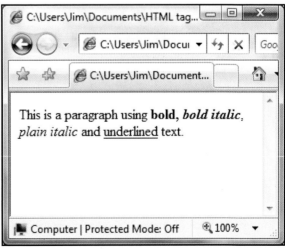

Left: Figure 1
Right: Figure 2

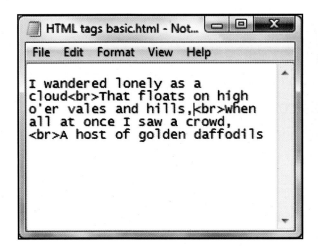

Left: Figure 3
Right: Figure 4
Below: Figure 5

bold, apply italics or change its colour. There's also an <em> tag, which defaults to italics. However, you can change its behaviour (as with any tag) using CSS. This is useful when you want two emphasis styles.

Having said that, browsers are perhaps the best example of how backwards-compatibility should work in software. Because they must still be able to render pages produced 10 or more years ago, even deprecated tags such as <u> still work, which means the pages you produce today should keep working well into the future.

The <p> and </p> tags in the example define the start and end of a paragraph. A web browser inserts a blank line after the </p> tag automatically. If you just want to move the cursor to the next line on the page so you can begin a fresh line without inserting a blank one between that and the text before it, use the tag <br> to insert a break.

As an example, to correctly lay out Wordsworth's poem *Daffodils* using the <br> tag, write the HTML shown in Figure 3. The result, when viewed in Internet Explorer 7, is shown in Figure 4 and correctly places each sentence of the poem on a new line.

PAGE OF REASON

Some tags apply not to specific sections of text but to a whole page, and they define where various structural sections begin and end. Again, they are always contained within angled brackets, opened and closed off using the same name in each instance but with a leading / before the closing tag, and never overlap.

The main page-wide tags, presented in the order in which they are applied, are shown in Figure 4, and must be used in every page you create. Most HTML editors provide these barebones of a web page for you.

As you can see, the <html> tag, which defines the very top and end of the file, surrounds all other tags. Within this, you have two main sections called <head> and <body>. Between <body> and </body>, as you can imagine, is where the main, visible content of your page will go.

The <head> tag is used for mainly administrative purposes. It tells the browser which character set to use when it renders the page. It tells search engines how they should index the page, and it tells any device that is capable of outputting the content (computer screen, smartphone, printer or screen reader for the visually impaired) how that content should be styled.

The <head> section also contains the <title> tag. Anything you enter between that and </title> will be displayed in the bar at the top of a browser, on the tab in any browser that is capable of opening more than one page at a time, in browser history lists and in the list of results returned by a search engine.

Give careful thought to what you include here. It's good practice to include your site name at the beginning so it is visible even if your visitor has several tabs open at once. It's also worth including a number of key phrases that relate specifically to the individual page to which it is attached, to make it stand out in search results. So, in our holiday cottage example, you could use the code:

```
<title>Redcot Barn | memorable family
breaks in Shakespeare country</title>
```

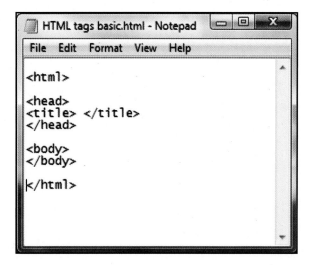

Formatting tags

It's vital that you format the words on your web pages correctly, or else visitors will struggle to navigate the site and may look elsewhere

Below: Basic HTML tags for headline formatting and adding emphasis should render identically in any browser, as seen here in IE7 and Firefox

As we've already explained, the simplest web page can consist of nothing more than a line of text tapped out on a blank page. Although this is the fastest way to convey a limited amount of information, it lacks structure, which is essential for guiding your visitor around the page and defining a hierarchy of importance. HTML is well suited to this task.

On page 50 we covered the tags `<b>`, `<i>` and `<u>`, which deal with bolding, italicising and underlining text, and we showed you how these tags can be combined to build up a range of effects.

HTML also has a range of pre-defined header styles, which use the tags `<h1>` to `<h7>`. Any text that is wrapped inside one of these tags (such as `<h1>`) and closed off with a matching tag with a leading / (such as `</h1>`) will be treated as a separate paragraph, and will have a blank line added beneath it. You can see from the images below how these headings look in their default state in Internet Explorer (left) and Mozilla Firefox (right). In Chapter 4, we'll show you how headings can be tailored to your specific needs.

HAPPY FAMILIES

Every browser has a default font setting. This can be defined by the user through the browser preferences. Unless you override it in your code, the setting will be used to display any unstyled text on your pages. You can specify your own font settings using the font tag. This can have a range of variables attached to it – including font face, size and colour – to tailor the style of the text to which it has been applied. It works like this:

```
<font face="Arial" size="-1"
 color="red">
```

American spellings are common in HTML; notice how the word 'colour' is spelt without a 'u'. The face command specifies the name of the font that should be used. In the example above we've used Arial, but this will rely on the visitor's computer having that font installed. There is no way you can guarantee this, so it is usual to specify a range of similar fonts separated by commas, such as 'Arial, Helvetica, sans serif'. When your visitor's browser loads the page, it will read through this list and use the first one it comes to that is installed on its system.

Say your preference is for Helvetica, with Arial as a fallback for people who don't have Helvetica installed. In this case, reverse the order so the tag starts:

```
<font face="Helvetica, Arial,
 sans-serif"...
```

Other commonly used families are as follows:

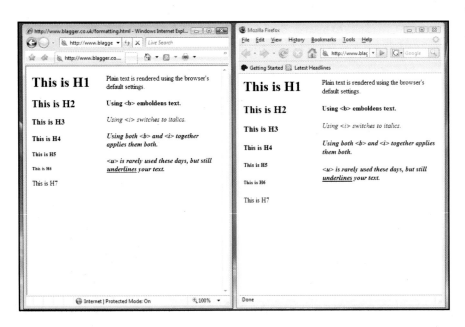

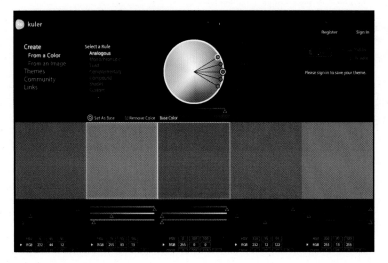

Red colors / Pink colors / Orange colors

HTML name	Hex code R G B	Decimal code R G B
Red colors		
IndianRed	CD 5C 5C	205 92 92
LightCoral	F0 80 80	240 128 128
Salmon	FA 80 72	250 128 114
DarkSalmon	E9 96 7A	233 150 122
LightSalmon	FF A0 7A	255 160 122
Crimson	DC 14 3C	220 20 60
Red	FF 00 00	255 0 0
FireBrick	B2 22 22	178 34 34
DarkRed	8B 00 00	139 0 0
Pink colors		
Pink	FF C0 CB	255 192 203
LightPink	FF B6 C1	255 182 193
HotPink	FF 69 B4	255 105 180
DeepPink	FF 14 93	255 20 147
MediumVioletRed	C7 15 85	199 21 133
PaleVioletRed	DB 70 93	219 112 147
Orange colors		
LightSalmon	FF A0 7A	255 160 122
Coral	FF 7F 50	255 127 80
Tomato	FF 63 47	255 99 71

Green colors

HTML name	Hex code R G B	Decimal code R G B
GreenYellow	AD FF 2F	173 255 47
Chartreuse	7F FF 00	127 255 0
LawnGreen	7C FC 00	124 252 0
Lime	00 FF 00	0 255 0
LimeGreen	32 CD 32	50 205 50
PaleGreen	98 FB 98	152 251 152
LightGreen	90 EE 90	144 238 144
MediumSpringGreen	00 FA 9A	0 250 154
SpringGreen	00 FF 7F	0 255 127
MediumSeaGreen	3C B3 71	60 179 113
SeaGreen	2E 8B 57	46 139 87
ForestGreen	22 8B 22	34 139 34
Green	00 80 00	0 128 0
DarkGreen	00 64 00	0 100 0
YellowGreen	9A CD 32	154 205 50
OliveDrab	6B 8E 23	107 142 35
Olive	80 80 00	128 128 0
DarkOliveGreen	55 6B 2F	85 107 47
MediumAquamarine	66 CD AA	102 205 170
DarkSeaGreen	8F BC 8F	143 188 143

Brown colors / White colors

HTML name	Hex code R G B	Decimal code R G B
Brown colors		
Cornsilk	FF F8 DC	255 248 220
BlanchedAlmond	FF EB CD	255 235 205
Bisque	FF E4 C4	255 228 196
NavajoWhite	FF DE AD	255 222 173
Wheat	F5 DE B3	245 222 179
BurlyWood	DE B8 87	222 184 135
Tan	D2 B4 8C	210 180 140
RosyBrown	BC 8F 8F	188 143 143
SandyBrown	F4 A4 60	244 164 96
Goldenrod	DA A5 20	218 165 32
DarkGoldenrod	B8 86 0B	184 134 11
Peru	CD 85 3F	205 133 63
Chocolate	D2 69 1E	210 105 30
SaddleBrown	8B 45 13	139 69 19
Sienna	A0 52 2D	160 82 45
Brown	A5 2A 2A	165 42 42
Maroon	80 00 00	128 0 0
White colors		
White	FF FF FF	255 255 255
Snow	FF FA FA	255 250 250

Serif

Times New Roman

Times

Georgia

Sans-serif

Verdana

Arial

Helvetica

Geneva

Monospace

Courier New

Courier

SIZE ISN'T EVERYTHING

The `size=` attribute can be specified in several ways. In our example, we've said that the font should be one size smaller than the default on the visitor's browser. We could easily have stated '-2' for much smaller text, or '+2' to make it larger. However, this doesn't give you complete control over your page, and because you don't know how your visitor's browser is set up you can't be sure how the text will look on their screen.

For this reason, you may want to use pixel sizes for greater control. Just be careful when doing so. Ideally, you should apply pixel sizes only to items that absolutely must be styled in a specific way, such as entries in a menu that have to line up with one another. Your visitors may have set up their browser in a certain way because they have a visual impairment. If that's the case, they will not thank you for reducing the size of the main body of words on your page, thereby rendering it illegible for them. Remember, anything that makes your pages hard to read will send your visitors straight back to Google and on to your competitors.

If you do choose to use pixel sizes, you should structure your code as follows, replacing the size attribute with whatever you consider appropriate:

```
<font face="Arial, Helvetica,
 sans-serif" size="10px"...
```

COLOURFUL LANGUAGE

In our font setting example, we used a plain-English name for the font colour (`color="red"`). It is one of 147 colours to have been blessed with a name as well as the hexadecimal code used for other colours. You can find a list of colours at http://en.wikipedia.org/wiki/Web_colors#X11_color_names.

If the colour you want doesn't have a name, you must use the hexadecimal code. This specifies the quantity of red, green and blue that should be mixed to create that colour using the standard hexadecimal base. The base runs from 0 to 9 and also adds the letters A to F. The brightest possible colour on a computer screen is white, while the darkest is black, produced by turning off all colour. Black is represented using the code 000000.

All codes are six digits long, although it is sometimes possible to use a three-digit shorthand. The first two digits define the amount of red, the second pair defines the amount of green and the third pair the amount of blue used to make up the colour. The code 000000 tells the browser to use no red, no green and no blue when formatting the text to which it is applied. Knowing that the hexadecimal scale runs from 0 to F, and that white is at the opposite end of the scale to black, we can work out that white must be maximum red, maximum green and maximum blue – or, to use hexadecimal code, FFFFFF.

When used in the font tag, these colours are preceded by a hash (#). If we want a mid-grey rather than red and use a hexadecimal rather than a named colour, we write:

```
<font face="Arial, Helvetica, sans-
 serif" size="10px" color="#CCCCCC">
```

Adobe's Kuler application at http://kuler.adobe.com helps you choose colours that work well together, and specifies hexadecimal equivalents. See page 38 for details.

Left: Adobe's Kuler application helps you pick harmonious colours, and provides the hexadecimal codes used to render them correctly in a browser

Right: Many 'web-safe' colours have been given names that are easy to remember, so you don't have to resort to codes

Preparing images

The right images will add colour and meaning to your website — so choose them carefully and format them correctly before uploading

BENEFITS ● ● ●

- Understand file sizes, dimensions and compression
- Master the different file formats
- Learn how to place images on your pages

Imagine what a newspaper would look like without goal shots in its sports section or portraits of politicians and dignitaries in its news pages. Put bluntly, it would be dull, uninspiring and quickly passed by. So when putting together your website, it's worth remembering that images bring pages to life online just as they do in print.

However, while newspapers need the best possible picture quality, websites are a different matter. When you sign up for a hosting account, you rent server space from your provider. You're usually allowed a set bandwidth, which is a measure of the amount of data your visitors can download from your site. If you exceed it, you may incur a surcharge or have your site taken offline.

You need to limit your bandwidth usage as much as possible. The easiest way to do this is to compress the images on your site. Images take up far more space than

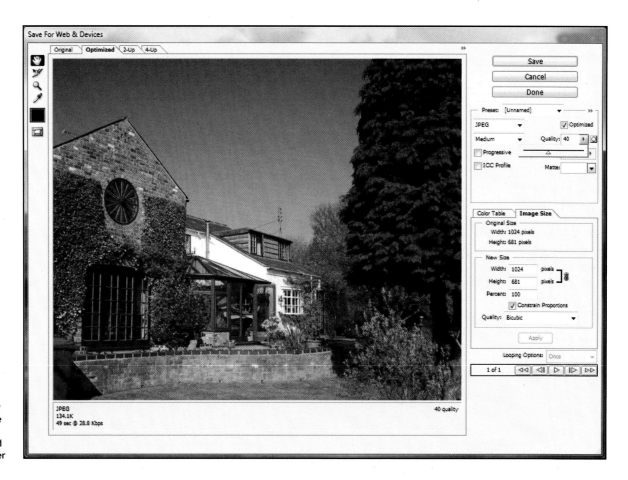

Right: Using photo-editing software to save web-friendly versions of images will reduce the amount of disk space and bandwidth they consume, and will lead to pages loading faster

words. Even the small pictures used by the BBC news site (http://news.bbc.co.uk) to illustrate a top story, usually taking up less than 20KB on disk, are the equivalent of downloading two A4-size pages of typed text. Compare this to a JPEG photo from an 8-megapixel digital camera, which could occupy around 2MB; this is over 100 times bigger. Clearly, you should never upload your photos straight from a camera's memory card.

Use your image-editing software's Save for Web feature – usually in the File menu – to export images with a suitable level of compression and in an appropriate file format. Photos should be saved as JPEGs, with quality set somewhere between 0 per cent and 100 per cent. The higher the quality level you choose, the lower the level of compression applied and the better the results, as the editing tool will preserve more data. The resulting file will be larger, though, and it will take longer to download and consume more bandwidth.

An image with a lot of flat colour, such as a logo or graphical button, should be saved as a PNG or GIF. These formats allow you to specify that some areas of the image should be transparent, so you can position images over a coloured background. GIF images can even be animated using the tools in many web graphics applications such as Adobe Fireworks.

However, you shouldn't rely on compression alone. Remember our mantra of planning ahead and sketching out your web pages, at least in your mind. Consider how much space your image will take up on the screen. This is measured in pixels rather than centimetres or inches, and should be used as a guide for shrinking your images, either by cropping them or changing their resolution. If you don't do this, you'll have to specify height and width manually, and if you end up downscaling images on the page you'll have wasted more of your precious bandwidth by having your visitors download huge images they'll never see in their full glory.

PUBLISHING YOUR PHOTOS

Once you've gathered your resized and compressed pictures into the images folder of your site, you can put them on to your pages (we'll show you how to upload files on page 60). The `<img>` tag that places images on a page takes several variables. However, unlike other tags, it isn't closed off by a matching `</img>` tag. The tag used to include a picture stored in the images folder of your site might look like this:

```
<img src="/images/kitchen.jpg"
  alt="Self-catering kitchen" width="450"
  height="337" border="0" align="left"
  hspace="5" vspace="10">
```

The top line is the only essential part of the image tag. The rest gives greater control over the use of the image, but if it is left out the image is still displayed. The

Left: The small images used to illustrate the lead story on the BBC's news website can take up as much server space as two pages of typewritten text

opening tag tells the browser it's working with an image, while `src` tells it that what follows is the source of the file. It's called kitchen.jpg and is stored in the images folder. The `images` part is preceded by a forward slash (`/`), which tells the browser to look in the root of the website's space on the server. It's advisable to use this method – rather than the full address of the image's location, such as www.redcotbarn.co.uk/images/kitchen.jpg – as it allows you to move the page to another folder on the site or re-use this line of code on another page.

The `alt="Self-catering kitchen"` part defines a tooltip that pops up when the visitor moves their mouse over the image, and is displayed within the image space before the image loads. If the image cannot be loaded, this line gives your visitors a clue as to what they are missing, so make it descriptive and helpful.

EXTRA DIMENSIONS

The `width=` and `height=` parameters define the image dimensions. Without them, the browser will use the image's size as it was saved from your camera or image editor. Specifying dimensions gives you more control, and tells the browser how much space to leave for the image on the page if it starts laying out your words before the image has finished loading.

Specifying `border="0"` determines the thickness of the border around the image. The amount will depend on how well you want the picture to blend into the page. If your pages have white backgrounds and your image features a cloudy or burnt-out sky, you may specify a border of 2 or 3. Specifying 0 means that if you use the image as a link by wrapping it in `<a>` tags (see page 56), it won't be surrounded by the default blue and purple borders used to denote new and visited links respectively.

The last three variables in the tag define how the image interacts with other elements on the page. Here we have set it to align with the left-hand margin; we could have set it to 'right' or 'center' (American spelling). We have also set a gap of five pixels left and right of the image, and 10 pixels above and below the image. This gives the image breathing space, and prevents words and other images on the page overlapping it.

Adding links

Any web page you create is only as effective as its links to the rest of the internet, so make sure you define your links correctly

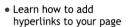

BENEFITS ●●●

- Learn how to add hyperlinks to your page
- Use text and images as links
- Make linked pages open in the same or different windows

Below left: The link to the Directions page opens in the same tab in the browser

Below right: This link opens the page in a new tab

If words and pictures are the flesh of your site, the links you use between pages on your site and those of others are the bones that hold things together and the joints that connect your site to the rest of the web.

The tag used to define a link is <a>, which stands for anchor. It is closed off by a matching tag that is preceded by a leading slash, </a>. Variables included as part of the opening <a> define the destination of the link, how it should be opened and to what it relates, while text or images used between this and the closing </a> become the elements on which visitors click to follow the link.

DROPPING ANCHOR

A typical link to another page on your site looks like this:

```
<a href="about.html" title="More
  information about Redcot Barn">
  About</a>
```

A link to an external site may look like this:

```
<a href="http://www.bbc.co.uk/news/"
  title="BBC Homepage" target="_blank">
  BBC homepage</a>
```

There are some subtle differences between the two. The first is in the address: while we are able to specify just the filename of the page that we want in our local site, we have to use the complete web address when pointing to external sites, and include the http:// at the beginning. If you were to just use www.bbc.co.uk, for example, the visitor's browser would look for a directory or file using that name on your own site and it would throw up an error when it couldn't find one.

The link on our local site assumes that the file about.html is stored in the same folder as the page from which we are linking to it. If it isn't, we need to include

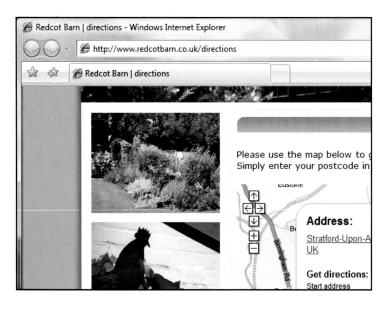

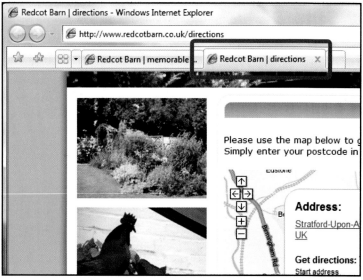

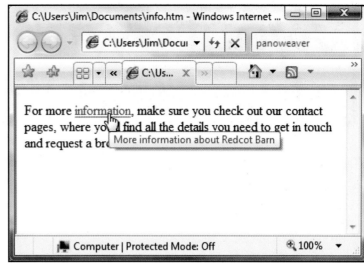

the folder where it can be found. Ideally, you should specify this in relation to the root of your web space, using the site map you drew in your planning stages. So, if we were coding a page to be saved at www.redcotbarn.co.uk/contact/index.html and wanted to link to a file called index.html located at www.redcotbarn.co.uk/about/index.html, we could use any of the following:

```
<a href="http://www.redcotbarn.co.uk/
  about/index.html"…
<a href="/about/index.html"…
<a href="/about/"…
<a href="../about/index.html"…
```

The first is self-explanatory; the second works because the forward-slash that opens the address tells the browser to go to the root of your website, dig down to the 'about' folder and from there open the file index.html. The third variant works because most web servers are programmed to open files with certain names whenever they find them in a folder and index.html is one such name (index.htm, index.shtml, index.php and default.html are others).

The final option will be familiar to anyone who uses the Linux command line, or used DOS before switching to Windows. The '..' tells the browser to move one level up the folder tree to the root and from there go into the folder called 'about' and load the file index.html.

In the links to both the local and remote files, we've included a 'title' variable. This works like a tooltip, with most browsers displaying it as your visitor hovers their mouse over the link. It is also used to help search engines properly index your site and the places to which it links. Carefully written titles here can do much to improve your standing in search results.

MEETING TARGETS

In the link to the remote site, we have included a 'target' variable. This tells the browser how to open the link. If you leave this out, the browser opens the link in place of your own page in the current page. Generally, this is what you should allow to happen, but there may be occasions when you want to have your own site remain open in one browser window while opening the link in another. Some modern browsers will open the site you reference with a `target="_blank"` tag in a new tab of the same window.

The `_blank` tells the browser to start a new, blank workspace for the link. Other targets that can be included here are `_self`, `_top` or `_parent`, but these usually relate to handling links in sites that use frames. As few sites use frames these days, and we recommend avoiding them wherever possible, they're not covered in detail here.

PUTTING THINGS IN CONTEXT

Once you've defined the destination of your link, you need to tell your visitor what they will find when they get there. Whether you're linking locally within your own site or to an external site such as the BBC, this is done by using the element that appears between the link definition that we've just covered and the closing `</a>` tag.

In the examples above, we've used a regular line of text (`About` and `BBC homepage` respectively). It could just as easily be a link to an image using the kind of image-positioning code outlined on page 55. In this case, you will almost certainly want to set your image's border variable to 0.

Links are flexible when it comes to positioning them, and you can include them within other tags, such as the H1 to H7 headline tags outlined on page 52, or around any complete element on the page, such as a CSS layer. Careful use of links, in combination with the CSS techniques we'll explain in the next chapter, will allow you to create some impressive and truly interactive web design with very little effort.

Above left: A link to a remote site, using the BBC homepage as the target in our example

Above right: A 'tool tip' link to a local file, with a carefully written title, can help search engines to index your site properly

Layouts with tables and lists

Tables and lists give your web pages definition, so it's important to get a good grasp of how they can help as layout tools

By now you should understand the fundamentals of web design and you should have a clear grasp of formatting text, placing images and creating links between various pages on your site, and to sites beyond your own domain. Now it's time to start thinking about how it should all sit on the page.

A decade ago, web designers used frames to split the visitor's browser windows into discrete sections and load a separate page into each. Times have moved on, and frames are now frowned upon. These days, most layouts are created using cascading style sheets, which we will cover in detail in the next chapter. Before we have a look at those, though, we need to understand another key layout tool: the table.

TURNING THE TABLES

You can use a table to structure your whole page, positioning images and text in its cells to keep them properly arranged. The cells can have coloured backgrounds, their contents can be set to align left, right or centre, their boundaries set to have borders and padding, and cells that should span more than one column or row can be merged to form wider or taller spaces.

The three key tags used to define a table are `<table>`, `<tr>` (table row) and `<td>` (table data cell). These are used in turn to describe the layout, working from the top down. Each one must be properly closed off with a matching tag that is preceded by a slash. While you can get away with missing the `</p>` off the end of a paragraph, forgetting the `</tr>` at the end of a table row or the `</td>` at the end of a cell will have disastrous consequences.

To explain how it works, we're going to use code to create the table in the screen here. The table has three rows and two columns, with the cells of the top row merged to create a header cell. As you can see from the code on the page opposite, the whole table is formed between the `<table>` and `</table>` tags. Each row of cells comes between `<tr>` and `</tr>`, and the contents of each cell are between `<td>` and `</td>`. We have centred the text inside each cell by attaching the variable `align="center"` to the `<td>` tags and stretched the only cell in the top row across both columns using the variable `colspan="2"`. If we hadn't done this then the browser would have been unable to render the table correctly, as all rows must contain the same number of cells, and we would have defined just one in the top row.

However, merged cells do not need to cross the whole of a table from one side to the other. If the rows below our top row had each been made up of three cells rather than two, we could have merged two cells into one on the top row and included another cell either before or after the two merged cells, so the total still added up to three – the number of cells in the rows below.

THE HARD CELL

We've applied some formatting to the whole table in the opening `<table>` tag. A one-pixel border will be drawn

Right: A simple HTML table, with two cells in the top row merged into one

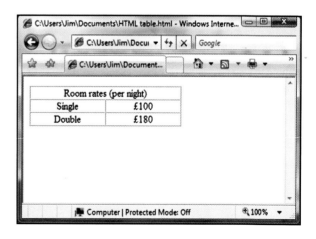

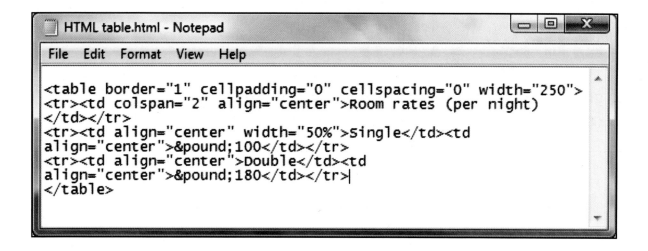

```
HTML table.html - Notepad
File  Edit  Format  View  Help
<table border="1" cellpadding="0" cellspacing="0" width="250">
<tr><td colspan="2" align="center">Room rates (per night)
</td></tr>
<tr><td align="center" width="50%">Single</td><td
align="center">&pound;100</td></tr>
<tr><td align="center">Double</td><td
align="center">&pound;180</td></tr>
</table>
```

around each cell, plus the table perimeter. We've chosen to remove all padding between the contents of the cells and their borders, and all the spacing that would, by default, appear between each cell in the table. Finally, we've fixed the table's width at 250 pixels.

Each of the individual table cells, apart from those at the top that have been set to span both columns, take up half the width of the table. We've specified that the first individual cell, which appears in the left-hand column of the second row, is 50 per cent in width, or half the width of the full table. All remaining cells in that column must be the same width. As there are only two columns, the cells in the second column must balance out the width and so use the other half of the width.

Instead of using the £ symbol on our table, we are using the code £. This ensures greater compatibility with the widest range of browsers and language settings, as you cannot know for sure that your visitors' browsers will correctly display the pound sterling symbol if used as a character. Similar codes can be used to define a non-breaking space ( ), copyright (©), a quarter (¼), a half (½) and three-quarters (¾).

MAKING LISTS

Lists work in a similar way to tables. It's easiest to think of them as a single-column table. Each entry in a list can be preceded by a bullet or a number. Bulleted lists are termed unordered and are initiated using the tag <ul>, while lists with leading numbers are termed ordered and initiated using <ol>. Each entry in a list is marked out using the tag <li> for list item, whether you're working with ordered or unordered lists. To see how this works, enter the following code and preview the results in your browser, then replace the <ol> and </ol> with <ul> and </ul> to swap the numbers for bullets:

```
<b>Redcot Barn house rules</b>
<ol>
<li>No pets</li>
<li>No smoking inside the building</li>
<li>No loud music after 11pm</li>
<li>Please tidy up after yourself</li>
</ol>
```

We've arranged the two lists side by side, as you can see in the screen below.

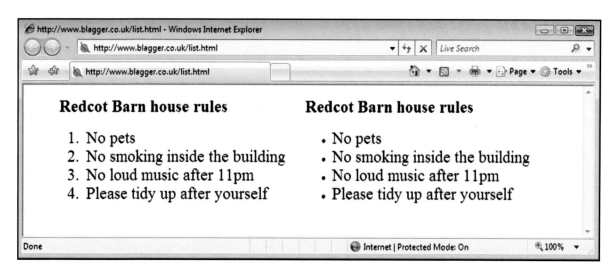

Top: The HTML code for our simple table

Bottom: Bulleted and numbered lists are almost identical in coding, but differ greatly when rendered on screen

Uploading your site

Once you've got to grips with all the main page elements and how they fit together, you're ready to prepare your website for publishing

You now have all the tools you need to build a website. As long as you remember that, with few exceptions, every tag you open must end with a matching tag with a preceding /, you won't go far wrong. Start simply and work up to more complex designs as your confidence increases. The next chapter will help you gain more control over your designs.

You can now publish your website. Usually, you upload your website's files using file transfer protocol (FTP) software, which sends your files to the server that will host them. It can also be used to retrieve files without them being rendered as web pages, so you get the raw structure saved to your hard disk for editing later.

You may be tempted to send all your pages and images to the server and then delete them from your hard disk, but you should avoid this, even if you're running short on space. Although reputable web hosts back up their servers regularly, you need to take equal responsibility for your work, as few will accept the blame if your only copy goes missing.

Below left: CuteFTP
Below middle: CoffeeCup Free FTP
Below right: Cyber Duck

FTP TOOLS

Your web host may give you FTP software with your hosting package, or it might employ server-side tools such as Plesk, which allow you to publish your work through a browser. If neither of these options is open to you, then a wide range of both paid-for and free tools can be downloaded from the following sources:

CuteFTP

www.cuteftp.com/cuteftp
This is one of the most popular tools available, with a large user base. The home edition allows a 30-day trial, after which registration costs $40 (around £20).

CoffeeCup Free FTP

www.coffeecup.com/free-ftp
As its name suggests, this tool is free, but it has all the features you would expect of an FTP client. As such, it's the one that we've used in our guide to publishing your pages (opposite).

Cyber Duck

www.cyberduck.ch
It may have a strange name, but this is the best FTP software available for Mac users. This donation-ware allows you to drag and drop files from the desktop or finder windows to your web server.

How to... Upload files with CoffeeCup Free FTP

Before you upload anything to your server, you'll need some details from your web host: your username and password, the address of the server and the directory into which you must upload files. The address may be as simple as ftp.[yourdomainname].co.uk or as general as uploads.[yourhost].co.uk.

1 Launch CoffeeCup and click the Servers button. Click the '+' on the dialog box that appears. Fill in the table that stores your server data. Give your connection a memorable name to differentiate it from other connections you might set up. The server name, username and password will all have been provided by your host. Leave the Passive box unticked unless your host has told you to use Passive FTP. Click the More Options button and enter the folder on your hard disk in which you have saved your files in the Local Folder box, and the folder on the server into which your host told you to upload them in the Remote Folder box.

2 Save your settings to exit the dialog box. Click the drop-down arrow beside the Servers button. This will list all the servers you have set up; pick the one you've just specified. Assuming you entered the right settings, CoffeeCup connects to the server and displays a list of your locally saved pages and files in the upper-left window of its interface, and the files on your server in the upper-right window. If there are any folders with names such as index.html, index.htm, index.php or default.html in the right-

hand window, delete them by right-clicking and selecting Delete. Leaving them where they are may mean they load instead of your own site if your new files don't overwrite them.

3 If you didn't specify a local folder when setting up the server connection, click in the address box above the left-hand window and type it, or click through the directory structure in the window itself to navigate to your files. Select all your files using Ctrl-A, or Ctrl-click individual files to select those you want to put online. Then click the Upload button on the toolbar. CoffeeCup will send your files to the server where they will be made live. Ensure that you have uploaded all the files that your site needs, including any that may be stored in subfolders, such as images.

4 Visit your site in a web browser. If you've uploaded the files to the root of your server space rather than to a hidden development folder that casual visitors will never find, they are now online for all to see, and you should check that they appear as expected. If you spot any problems, go back immediately and take remedial action. Don't leave them online with the intention of doing it later; you have no way of knowing how many people may see them in the meantime, and if your pages are designed to promote your business they will have precisely the opposite effect if they are littered with spelling mistakes, have empty image boxes or don't render correctly in every browser.

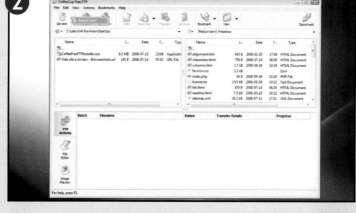

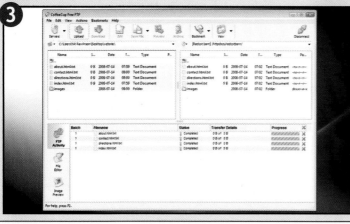

Using CSS

While you can use HTML exclusively on your website, it's far better to use Cascading Style Sheets, or CSS. This sounds impressive, but it simply defines the way your website looks. CSS is distinct from HTML, and a simple change to one file could completely transform the way your site looks. CSS also allows you far more precision and control over page layout, and provides some clever tricks to make your site look great.

In this chapter, we'll explain how CSS works and how you can use it to produce a three-column page layout and an interactive menu bar that doesn't require the use of a graphics application.

As with the HTML examples used in the last chapter, special software isn't required to use CSS: Windows' Notepad editor is all you need.

Understanding CSS

If you want your website to have consistency and clarity, and you want to reduce the work involved in changing styles, CSS will prove invaluable

BENEFITS ● ● ●

- Get an overview of the benefits of CSS
- Learn how to keep the CSS code separate from the HTML

Cascading Style Sheets (CSS) can mean different things to different people. To some, CSS is the web-design equivalent of desktop publishing, providing far more precise control over the look and feel of a website than HTML alone. To others, it's the future of web design, providing the ability to add special effects that were previously impossible. To most people, though, it's the quickest, most widely compatible way of producing stunning online designs. CSS reduces the work involved in designing a website, enabling users to recycle their work and ensuring consistency across an entire site. It's easy to see why this language is becoming a standard.

THE PROBLEM WITH HTML

HTML is great for defining the underlying structure of a web page, and it offers a set of rudimentary styling tags. As we showed in Chapter 3, it includes tables for organising and aligning your content, and lets you tweak the appearance of photos and text, either case by case or across your entire page. However, it doesn't go as far as many would like.

Styling tags must often be applied to each element individually, so if you have a 15-paragraph page styled in Arial and you want to switch to Verdana, you'll have to make 15 changes to your code to get the job done. This is time-consuming and increases the risk of introducing errors and inconsistencies into your code.

As these tags are scattered throughout your code, it means that it's harder for less experienced users to make amendments, because the page's structural information and its actual content are muddled together.

STYLE CHALLENGE

CSS addresses these shortcomings. By separating these elements, a group of developers working as a team can assign styling tasks to a coding expert, while a writer works on the content. CSS offers a far greater range of options for styling your content and laying it out with pixel-perfect precision. It also simplifies many tasks, such as defining layouts. Rather than defining a clumsy table with columns, rows and cells, you need only specify where a box of content should begin and end, and how big it should be.

CSS code is infinitely flexible, allowing you to define how elements – such as links using the <a> tag, pictures using the <img> tag or headings using the <h1> tag – look across an entire website. Alternatively, you can give each element a unique name and assign it an individual style that doesn't appear anywhere else on your site.

Although you can write the CSS code directly into your page, the real benefit comes in separating it into a file of its own. With the style information separated from the content, you can focus your attention on producing excellent copy for your visitors to read when working with the pages themselves, and switch to a more visual mindset when it comes to defining the layout.

When you separate CSS in this way, you call it into each page with a single line of code in the <head> section. This means you can create a single stylesheet for your entire site, to which each page refers in turn. The benefit is obvious: by centralising your style and layout information in a single file that all your pages use as a resource, you can make radical site-wide changes simply by editing the stylesheet rather than having to change every individual page on your site. As a result, you will spend less time working on the code for each page, and reduce the chance of introducing errors in the process.

Professional web designers use CSS widely, and if you're serious about developing your website, you should make the effort to learn at least the basics. Fortunately you don't need to do this wholesale from day one. As we explained on page 51, browsers are a perfect example of how all software should handle backwards-compatibility, as they are happy to mix 10-year-old code with the latest CSS mark-up.

When you start using CSS to style your layouts, we recommend that you use layers rather than tables and, if you wish, stick with the HTML formatting tags we defined in the previous section before moving on from there. We also recommend that you work with elements that already exist within HTML, such as <h1>, <h2>, <p> and others, so that any visually impaired visitors who have defined their own stylesheet can apply that in preference to your own CSS mark-up if they find your choices difficult to read.

GETTING STARTED

CSS is most often applied to web pages, but you can use it to define the style of any XML-based document, including some graphics files. You can also use it to specify output devices, which means you can apply more than one stylesheet to your page and ask the browser to use the most appropriate one for the device on which it is running. With three stylesheets running in tandem, for example, you could produce specific pages for a regular PC screen, a portable device such as a PDA or Windows Mobile-based phone and even a printer, which would set

```
Untitled - Notepad
File  Edit  Format  View  Help
<head>
<title>Welcome to Redcot Barn</title>
<style type="text/css">
<!--
body {
                behavior:url("csshover.htc");
        }
#container {
        width: 960px;
        margin-right: auto;
        margin-left: auto;
        text-align:left;
}
        #menu {
        float: left;
        width: 150px;
        margin-right: 10px;
}
#content {
        float: left;
        width: 590px;
}
#sidebar {
        float: right;
        width: 200px;
}
#footer {
        border-top: 1px solid #000000;
        clear: both;
        margin-left: 160px;
        padding-top: 10px;
}
-->
</style>
<!--
#widemenu ul li {
        float: left;
        list-style-type: none;
        padding-right: 30px;
        padding-left: 5px;
        padding-bottom: 5px;
        padding-top: 5px;
        font-family: Arial, Helvetica, sans-serif;
        font-weight: bold;
        font-size: 14px;
        display: block;
}
#widemenu {
        background-color: #dddddd;
        margin-bottom: 10px;
        height: 25px;
}
#widemenu ul li a {
        color: #000000;
        text-decoration: none;
        display: block;
}
#widemenu ul li:hover {
        background-color: #bbbbbb;
        display: block;
}
#widemenu ul {
        height: 8px;
        margin: 0px;
        padding: 0px;
        display: block;
}
-->
</head>
```

Left: Separating the style information from the content makes designing your website easier and more versatile

the page up for the optimum reproduction on paper rather than on a screen.

Unfortunately, not all browsers are the same, and the more you use CSS, the more you will see that Internet Explorer's interpretation of your code can vary widely from those of the other major (and minor) browsers, which render web pages similarly.

Over the next few pages, we'll show you how to get round some of these problems. Once you take things further, though, you may have to start applying special conditional classes that interrogate the browser and change the way an element is implemented on the page. There are so many different instances when you may need to do this that they merit a book of their own. We can't cover them in full here, but an online search for 'IE conditional CSS' will provide a wealth of results.

Applying the basics

CSS is complicated, but you can start using the basics straight away. Here we show you how to get started with this versatile language

It can help to think of CSS as a plain-English description of how elements on your page should look. The styles are split up according to the elements to which they apply. This can affect anything from a single item on your page to every tag of a certain style. Here we'll show you how to define a range of common styles using CSS, and how to apply those styles to your pages.

YOUR FIRST STYLE SHEET

Styles can be applied on a page-by-page basis and are defined within the head section of a page between a series of special characters that, in effect, turns styles into a comment. In this way the browser reads the instructions as the page loads, but they won't appear on the page itself.

If we were to use this method to embed CSS code that gives our page a grey background, we would insert this section between the `<head>` and `</head>` tags:

```
<style type="text/css">
<!--
body {
    background-color: #CCCCCC;
}
-->
</style>
```

The `<!--` and `-->` lines define a section of your page that the browser should treat only as information. It could be a note you've written to yourself, a section of code that you want to remove temporarily from the page without actually deleting or, as in this case, the place where you define your CSS attributes.

However, this is only a partial solution to the problems we outlined in the opening part of this section on CSS. While we have separated the styling information

from the actual content of the page, we are still including it in the page itself, at the very top.

A far more efficient method is to define the look of your page in a separate file – a dedicated stylesheet – which you then attach to your page by adding a line to its header section. This way, you can call the same stylesheet into every page on your site, ensuring greater consistency and saving you the task of changing the styles on every page in your site when you want to freshen it up. The code for calling a stylesheet into your page looks like this:

```
<head>
<title>This is the title of my page
  </title>
<link href="styles.css" rel="stylesheet"
```

```
type="text/css">
</head>
```

Here you're telling the page to use a stylesheet called styles.css. The browser knows this is stored in the same folder as the page on which you are working, as no directory information is included.

Like web pages, stylesheets can have any name you choose. You can also link several stylesheets to a single page by giving them different names, calling them in by repeating the `<link` line above as many times as you need and swapping out the `"styles.css"` part. This way, you can have a single master stylesheet that you use across your site, and several tailored sheets that apply to individual pages.

STYLES FOR LAYOUT

When switching to CSS, you also need to start coding your pages differently. You can mix and match old and new technology, but while you can still use tables to define your layout, you should really use them only for tabular data – such as timetables and small spreadsheets within your pages – and switch to using layers for the actual guts of the layout. These layers are defined using the `<div>` tag, and can be sized and positioned with just as much precision as a text or picture box in DTP.

Your page will have several layers, and each one needs a name so that you can target it precisely with the appropriate style. If we were working on a page called about.html, we might want to include a layer called menu, like this:

```
<div id="menu">Layer content goes
  here.</div>
```

We can now style it in our stylesheet:

```
#menu {
    background-color: #FFFF99;
    margin: 10px;
    padding: 5px;
    height: 300px;
    width: 450px;
    border: 4px dotted #333333;
}
```

This turns our layer into a text or picture frame 450x300 pixels in size, with a 10-pixel margin around the edge to stop other page elements butting up against it. It has a yellow background (FFFF99) and a four-pixel-wide border made up using dark grey (333333) dots. Looking at the code above, you can probably see how easily you could tweak this to meet your own needs.

As you can see, the style name in our stylesheet (#menu) is the same name we have given to the layer in

the file about.html, with the addition of the leading #. The hash tells the browser to apply this style only to layers of that name. This means we can use the name 'menu' again elsewhere for elements that are not layers.

You can also see that the styling information is contained between the { and } brackets and that each line ends with a semicolon. Make sure you follow both conventions when creating your own stylesheets, or your styling won't work.

TARGETTING STYLES

Just as we can isolate layers, we can also target specific elements in the general content of our pages. Imagine we have a long track of flowing text that we want to break up. We don't have any images at our disposal, so we'll use a pullquote to highlight an interesting point in the text. To do this, we would include the following code in our about.html page:

```
<p class="pullquote">My really important
  words go here</p>
```

As we want to use this text in the middle of a piece of flowing copy and we don't want to break it up with a new layer `<div>`, we have applied the new style only to a specific paragraph in the text by attaching a class that we will define in the stylesheet. We can use the class, called pullquote, with as many paragraphs as we like on any of the pages to which we have attached the stylesheet, ensuring a consistency of style throughout the website.

The formatting for the pullquote is defined in the stylesheet as follows:

```
.pullquote {
    font: 18px Arial, Helvetica,
```

Below: By applying CSS styling that floats our text to the right and applies borders above and below, we can easily turn a regular paragraph into a pullquote around which the rest of the content on our pages will neatly flow

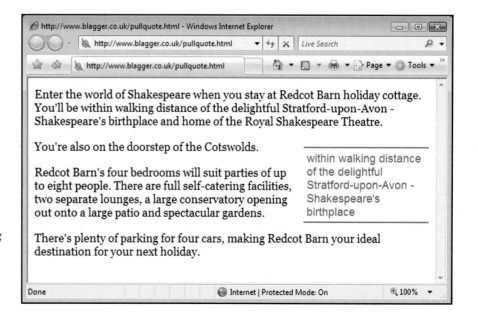

```
            sans-serif;
    color: #666666;
    width: 120px;
    margin: 10px 0px 10px 10px;
    padding: 5px;
    border-bottom: 2px solid #666666;
    border-top: 2px solid #666666;
    float: right;
}
...
```

The dot that precedes the class name (pullquote) indicates to the browser that it should apply its contents only to a specific element with that class attached to it, and not to any layers we might also call 'pullquote'. You may think you would never do this, but consider that in the 'menu' example above, you may have a style for your menu layer, and want to define separately the font used to display different menus on different pages.

Our styling code for the pullquote defines the virtual box that contains the quoted sentence, and the actual styling of the quote itself. The box is 120 pixels wide, and as we haven't defined a height it will stretch to accommodate the words we put into it. This is important, because if we plan to use it on several pages throughout the site, we can never be sure that our quotes will always be the same length.

The box has a dark grey, two-pixel-wide solid border above and below, but as we haven't defined a background colour, the colour of the page will show through. It's right-aligned (float: right;) so the rest of our text

Below: The full code for our web page with a pullquote is remarkably short, showing how simple CSS really is

will flow around it and, because we want to give it some breathing space, we have applied a 10-pixel margin above, below and to the left. We do this in the line margin: 10px 0px 10px 10px, which is an abbreviation of the commands margin-top: 10px; margin-right: 0px and so on, in a single line to save space. The individual measurements in the line work in a clockwise direction, so the 10px 0px 10px 10px part tells the browser to apply those measurements to the top, right, bottom and left sides respectively. You can use this method to apply borders, margins and alignment to almost any element on your page, including images, by attaching appropriate classes.

We've also applied five pixels of padding. Padding is positioned within the dimensions of any layer; it is the area around an element. Here we're using it to keep the words away from the edges of the box.

The text is rendered in the same grey as the border and in 18-pixel Arial, Helvetica or sans serif, depending on which is installed on the visitor's computer.

CHANGING DEFAULT TAGS

You can use your stylesheet to make fundamental changes to the look of default HTML tags, such as paragraphs <p>, list items <li> or links <a>. You do this in the same way, but instead of giving each a name, you simply use its tag as the class name and drop the leading # or dot. For example:

```
.........
a {
    font-weight: bold;
    font-variant: small-caps;
    color: #990000;
    text-decoration: none;
}
...
```

This will make our links prominent by rendering them in small, bold, dark red capitals. It also removes the underline from each one.

CONDITIONAL STYLES

Using CSS rather than plain HTML for styling allows you to introduce interactive elements that would otherwise require the use of Flash or advanced programming skills. The simple addition of the :hover tag makes named elements aware of the position of your mouse, and causes them to act differently when you move your pointer over them. Designers often use this to change the way links look when you point at them.

The following code, for example, changes the links in our page to adopt an underline and turn green as the cursor moves over them:

```
.......................
a:hover {
    text-decoration: underline;
    color: #009900;
}
...
```

```
pullquote[1] - Notepad

File  Edit  Format  View  Help

<style type="text/css">
<!--
.pullquote {
        font: 18px Arial, Helvetica, sans-serif;
        color: #666666;
        width: 200px;
        margin: 10px 0px 10px 10px;
        padding: 5px;
        border-bottom: 2px solid #666666;
        border-top: 2px solid #666666;
        float: right;
}
.style1 {
        font-family: Georgia, "Times New Roman", Times, serif;
        font-size: 18px;
}
.style2 {
        font: 18px Arial, Helvetica, sans-serif;
        color: #666666;
        width: 200px;
        margin: 10px 0px 10px 10px;
        padding: 5px;
        border-bottom: 2px solid #666666;
        border-top: 2px solid #666666;
        float: right;
        font-family: Georgia, "Times New Roman", Times, serif;
        font-size: 18px;
}
-->
</style>
<p class="style1">Enter the world of Shakespeare when you stay at Redcot Barn
holiday cottage. You'll be within walking distance of the delightful Stratford-
upon-Avon - Shakespeare's birthplace and home of the Royal Shakespeare Theatre.</p>
<p class="pullquote">within walking distance of the delightful Stratford-upon-Avon
- Shakespeare's birthplace</p>
<p class="style1">You're also on the doorstep of the Cotswolds.</p>
<p class="style1">Redcot Barn's four bedrooms will suit parties of up to eight
people. There are full self-catering facilities, two separate lounges, a large
conservatory opening out onto a large patio and spectacular gardens.</p>
<p class="style1">There's plenty of parking for four cars, making Redcot Barn your
ideal destination for your next holiday.</p>
```

As you can see, we've defined only the parts that have changed, rather than writing out the entire style again from scratch. We've left the weight of the text (bold) and the case (small caps) unchanged from the original definition, as altering either of these would change the text's size on the page, and cause the text around it to shift position as your visitor moved their mouse around. If you've ever visited a website where this happens, you'll know how annoying it is.

So when a visitor's mouse pointer hovers over a link like this, the browser takes the style we have defined for `<a>` and uses it as the basis on which to make the changes detailed in `a:hover`.

Most browsers can apply a `:hover` state to any element on the page, allowing you to change not only links but also boxes, text areas, images and so on. However, Microsoft's Internet Explorer – which accounts for most of the browsing on almost all sites – restricts the use of `:hover` to links on a page. This means it's important not to rely on the `:hover` effect to such an extent that your content can be accessed only by users of browsers other than Internet Explorer, as we will show in the navigation bar example (page 76).

However, you can be even more specific in defining when certain styles apply to the various elements on your page. For example, you can style common features, such as lists, in different ways depending on where they appear within your page. This is another reason why you should make every effort to use layers rather than tables to lay out your pages.

GETTING TO THE POINT

As we will explain in greater detail on page 77, giving a full CSS description of the location of an element lets you restrict its effect to a single instance. For example, multi-level lists such as those you might use to outline points made in a meeting can have different bullet styles depending on whether the point made is a major point or just a sub-point of a bigger issue (or indeed a sub-point of that).

As we have already discovered, the HTML tag for defining a bulleted list is `<ul>`, and each entry within that list is defined using the tag `<li>`. To place a solid square next to the main points in the list, you would use the code:

```
ul li {
  list-style-type: square;
}
```

To define the bullets for subordinate points as small circles, which will be indented automatically, you would use the following:

```
ul li li {
  list-style-type: circle;
}
```

In effect, this tells the browser that for list items in an unordered list it should use square bullets, while for list items within list items within unordered lists it should use circles. You can go on adding further instances of li to the definition to target list items to an infinite degree within an ever-expanding list, although to be kind to your visitors we recommend breaking up your lists into more logical sections once they get deeper than two or three layers.

GOING FURTHER

Over the next eight pages, we are going to use CSS and a few other tools to create a classic three-column layout, which forms the basis of many websites. We'll then use this knowledge about interactivity to style up a list such as the one on page 59 as a menu for use throughout a site.

Above: Firebox is just one of millions of sites that use a classic three-column layout, which breaks the content up to make it easy to read

Putting CSS into practice

Creating the classic three-column layout favoured by modern web designers is quite straightforward with the help of CSS

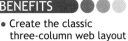

BENEFITS

- Create the classic three-column web layout
- Learn how to recycle this technique for use on other pages

A rmed with the basics of CSS that we've covered so far, we can use layers and a stylesheet to build a floating three-column layout. This is a classic of modern web design, allowing you to have a header at the top of the page, a menu in a narrow column on the left, a wide area in the middle of the page for the main content and another narrow column on the right that acts as a sidebar for adverts or supplementary information needed.

This type of design is relatively easy to create using just a few lines of CSS, but because different browsers work in different ways, we need to tweak the code to ensure that all browsers interpret it properly.

CREATING YOUR BASE FILES

To form our three-column design we'll take a basic HTML page and style it using CSS. To do this we need just a plain-text editor, such as Notepad, to create two files: index.html and styles.css. The index.html

Below: After entering text in the layers of our layout, it's easy to see how they all run together without any styling. We need to divide them into three distinct columns

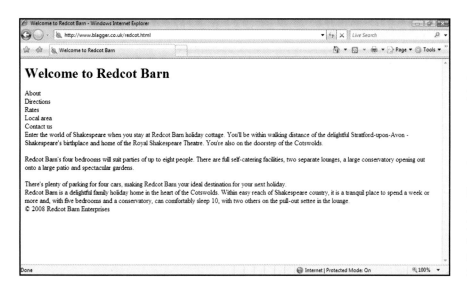

file will contain the content of the page, while the styles.css file will make it work.

It's worth typing in these examples, so you can get a real feel for how CSS works. The basic HTML page is the following short section of code:

```
<head>
<title>Welcome to Redcot Barn</title>
<link href="styles.css" rel="stylesheet"
 type="text/css">
</head>
<body>
<div id="container">
  <div id="header">Welcome to Redcot
   Barn</div>
  <div id="menu"></div>
  <div id="content"></div>
  <div id="sidebar"></div>
  <div id="footer"></div>
</div>
</body>
</html>
```

Believe it or not, that's the entire page. Everything we do from now on will be within the stylesheet. However, to make the different layers easier to differentiate onscreen, it's a good idea to enter some text into the menu, content and sidebar layers in the same way that we entered 'Welcome to Redcot Barn' in the header layer.

SETTING UP STYLES

As you can see from the code, the stylesheet for the page is defined within index.html. As it's stored in the same folder as the page itself, it's simply a case of specifying its name, rather than a full path to the folder in which it is saved.

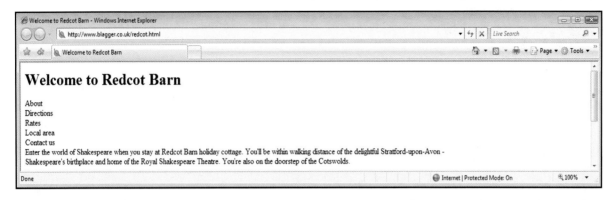

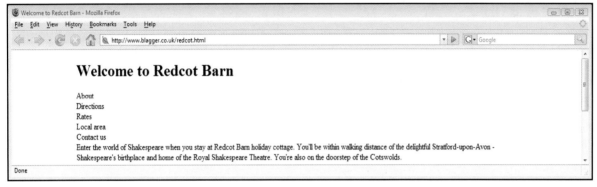

Left: Internet Explorer (top) renders centred layers differently to other browsers, as you can see when compared with Firefox (bottom)

As you don't know what screen resolution your visitors will be using, it's a good idea to design for nothing larger than 1,024 pixels in width. To allow room for scroll bars and application borders, you should confine your layout to a width of 960 pixels. Do this by defining a maximum size for the layer, called `container`, which contains every other layer on the page. You can then centre this onscreen by setting the margins on either side to `auto`, which tells the browser to split any unused width of the screen equally and position each half on either side of the layer. To do this, you have to add the following code to the file styles.css:

```
#container {
    width: 960px;
    margin-right: auto;
    margin-left: auto;
}
```

Again, the code is surrounded by { and } brackets, each line is terminated by a semicolon to show where the command ends, and a # is added to the front of the class name to apply it to a layer.

If you preview index.html in Firefox, you'll see that the container is indeed centred on the page. However, if you preview it in Internet Explorer it will stick stubbornly to the left-hand margin. This is because Explorer interprets the auto setting differently to other browsers when it's applied to the margins. Returning to styles.css, add the following, starting with a new line immediately below the } that closes the style:

```
body {
    text-align: center;
}
```

This centres everything on the page, including the container layer, which is what we want. Unfortunately, because it applies this formatting to the entire page and everything in any of the layers, it also centres the contents of the container. This is an unwanted side effect, as the text is now centred, which is not what we wanted. Returning to the styling for `#container` within styles.css, add the following line below `margin-left: auto;`:

```
text-align: left;
```

This will correct the text alignment in the container, and in any layers it holds. It does this because CSS allows styles to cascade from one section to any sections it contains, hence the name.

So, the browser loads the page and the stylesheet, extracts the styling for 'body', applies that to the entire page and then finds a layer called 'container'. It looks up the appropriate style for this (`#container`) and discovers that it overwrites the body commands within that section. It makes the necessary amendments to the text alignment until it gets to the end of the container layer and then switches back to the styling applied within 'body'. Anything you put on your page outside the container layer is centred unless you override that command again.

If you now preview index.html, you should see a properly formatted page in any browser, but it's still not a three-column layout. Assuming you have entered some text in your layers, you will see that they are stacked one above the other, and that each one stretches across the full width of the container.

We need to break up that width and apportion it to the various layers in our layout, giving the menu column 150 pixels, the sidebar 200 pixels and the main body copy 590 pixels. If you've been keeping count, you'll realise that this leaves us with 20 pixels spare, which we'll use to form two 10-pixel margins, one between the menu and the body, and the other between the body and the sidebar. The clever bit is that we'll define only one, and leave the browser to work out what to do with the other.

To begin, format the menu by adding this section of code on a new line immediately after the closing } in the body section of the stylesheet:

```
#menu {
    float: left;
```

Below: After styling the menu layer, we find that the text in the content layer flows around it like text in a newspaper flowing around a picture. It's easy to fix this by properly defining the content layer's dimensions

Bottom: The footer text is correctly positioned at the bottom of the page, but when we apply a border to the top edge, you can see that the footer layer actually starts immediately below the header

```
    width: 150px;
    margin-right: 10px;
}
```

This is fairly self-explanatory. It constrains the menu layer to a width of 150 pixels, applies a 10-pixel margin to the right-hand edge and floats it as close to the left of the container layer as it can. If you preview index.html in your browser now, you'll see that the content layer has jumped up to the top of the container layer and sits immediately below the header, alongside the menu. If you've entered enough text in this layer, it will flow down and around the menu like text running around a picture or a quote in a magazine.

We are going to fix this by styling the central content column in a similar way to the menu, adding the following immediately below the code for the #menu layer:

```
#content {
    float: left;
    width: 590px;
}
```

The styling information for the #content layer is even simpler than that for the #menu layer, even though it forms the main body of our page. Again, we have floated the layer to the left, but this time, because the #menu layer is also floated to the left and is in the way of the content column, the content can't get to the very left of the container. So its full 590-pixel width sits 160 pixels into the container, having been pushed there by the 150 pixels of the menu and the 10 pixels of the margin attached to the menu layer.

We'll now position the sidebar, and you'll see why we didn't include a margin to the right of the content layer. Add the following code to the styles.css file, immediately after the section defining #content:

```
#sidebar {
    float: right;
    width: 200px;
}
```

This fixes the width of the sidebar to 200 pixels and floats it to the right of the #container layer. A simple calculation shows where the margin between the sidebar and the content layer has come from: the menu was 150 pixels wide with a 10-pixel margin, and the content was 590 pixels wide. Adding them together, the total is 750 pixels. Subtract that from the width of the container – 960 pixels – and you're left with 210, which is 10 pixels wider than we need to contain the sidebar. Floating the sidebar to the right, therefore, creates a 10-pixel gap between its left-hand edge and the right-hand edge of the content layer.

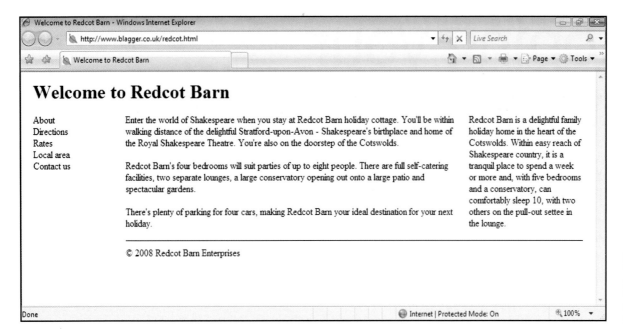

Now we just need to style the footer, which poses another interesting problem. We obviously want the footer to sit immediately beneath everything else in the container layer. However, if we add a top border to it using the following code, you'll see that while the text may have been pushed down by our other layers, the actual footer itself starts above them. Only its contents are pushed down:

```
#footer {
    border-top: 1px solid #000000;
}
```

This line adds a solid border (you could also use a dotted line, a dashed line or other options by substituting the word 'solid') one-pixel wide in black, which we specify here using the hexadecimal code #000000, as explained in more detail on page 55. If you now save the stylesheet and preview index.html, you'll see that while the line of text in the footer appears below the menu, content and sidebar layers, the upper border has become detached and appears above them.

To get round this problem, we need to tell the browser to keep the entire footer layer – including the border – clear of everything that comes before it by adding the following line above the closing } of the #footer definition shown above:

```
clear: both;
```

Save your stylesheet and preview index.html again and you should now see that the text and border have been united at the foot of the container layer, precisely where they should be. It's still not perfect, so shunt it in by 160 pixels from the left to line it up with the edge of the content layer. Give the text some breathing space by adding some internal padding to the top of the layer by completing the #footer styling as follows:

```
#footer {
    border-top: 1px solid #000000;
    clear: both;
    margin-left: 160px;
    padding-top: 10px;
}
```

RECYCLING YOUR LAYOUTS

Your layout is complete, and you can concentrate on styling the text and image content of those layers using the CSS elements explained at the start of this chapter, or the HTML commands outlined in Chapter 3.

Having established your stylesheet, you can easily re-use it elsewhere on your site by attaching it to other pages that are made using layers with the same names as those we have used for index.html. The immediate benefit is that you've halved the work of creating your new page, as the styles have already been defined.

This is small-fry, however, compared with what happens when you later decide to introduce an entirely new design across your website. As all the pages in your site use the same stylesheet, and each is structured using layers with matching names, you need to edit only a single file – styles.css – to apply your desired changes across the entire site. Suddenly what you may have imagined to be a several-day job that needed extensive planning and dedication can be completed in an hour or less, enabling you to concentrate on what really matters: creating compelling content that will have your visitors coming back time and again.

Developing your layout further

If you don't want your pages to have black text on a white background, you can add colours and effects with a little extra CSS

BENEFITS ●●●
- Make your pages look attractive by using coloured layers
- Find out how to use CSS for background images, including gradients and fades

You now know how to create a well-structured, familiar layout. Your visitors will see your three-column layout and feel immediately at home, having seen other examples all over the web. The only trouble is that this one is dull.

Adding colours, images and textures to layers can make them more inviting. Compare Google news (http://news.google.co.uk) with Sky News (http://news.sky.com), for example, and look at how Sky's use of coloured backgrounds makes its site look far more appealing than the strait-laced, text-based Google alternative.

We'll do something similar here to brighten up the design for Redcot Barn, still working solely with the stylesheet and never touching our HTML page.

ASSIGNING COLOURS TO LAYERS

Giving the page a coloured background is easy. We simply tweak the CSS that handles the body tag, which we used earlier to remedy Internet Explorer's problems in centring the container layer.

We'll give the page a light green wash, bringing to mind the countryside that surrounds our holiday home.

To do this, we'll rewrite the body section as follows:

```
body {
  text-align:center;
  background-color: #9EC7A0;
}
```

Now everything, including each of the layers, has a green background (#9EC7A0). We don't want this in the container layer, which should revert to white, so change the styling of #container as follows:

```
#container {
  width: 960px;
  margin-right: auto;
  margin-left: auto;
  text-align:left;
  background-color: #FFFFFF;
  padding: 5px;
}
```

This adds a pure white background and five pixels of

Right: Compare Sky's and Google's news services and you can see how adding some graphical backgrounds can make a page more appealing

padding around each side of the container layer. We added the padding because the menu, sidebar, header and footer were butting against the edges of the layer, and sitting uncomfortably against the green background. Adding five pixels of padding all round increases the overall width of the container layer by 10 pixels, to a total of 970, but this will still easily fit on a 1,024-pixel-wide display with room to spare.

ASSIGNING IMAGES TO LAYERS

Using images as backgrounds is just as easy. First, make sure they are properly sized and compressed. If you are using a photo as a background, you must also reduce its opacity so that the sharp contrasts don't interfere with the legibility of your overlying text.

However, image backgrounds don't have to be photos. Using subtle graphical elements such as fades and rounded corners can often be more effective, and give your layout depth. Look at how MSN has used this to good effect at http://uk.msn.com, where a light blue background slowly fades out behind the main body of the page, and the sidebar to the right uses a graduated tint that fades smoothly from blue to white and back to blue.

We can easily do something similar to our design by using a light green background that fades to white behind our main #content section. This will help it stand out between the two white sidebars. The best way to do this is to create a narrow image which is then tiled across the full width of the layer. Because both the left and right sides of this image will be identical, we can make it very narrow. All we need is a thin strip just five pixels wide and 300 pixels tall that's solid green at the top and fades to white at the bottom. Save this as bgfade.gif in the same folder as the page.

Image backgrounds are designed to fill the entire background of a layer, regardless of its size, so they tile vertically as well as horizontally. This is a problem, as our graphic is designed to appear only at the top of the #content layer. As it starts out at 100 per cent strength and fades to nothing, it would look terrible if it then reappeared at full strength again immediately below the point at which it disappeared. We will therefore need to restrict its repetition to just the horizontal plane and not the vertical, which we can do with the line `background-repeat: repeat-x;`. If you wanted to repeat an image only on the vertical axis, you'd put a 'y' where the 'x' is. If you don't want any repetition at all, use `background-repeat: no-repeat;`.

With a background image in place, you need to consider how it will look behind some text. In our example, the text starts at the far left of the layer and runs across the very top. This was fine when there was no background, but now it would look uncomfortably tight. As such, we must add some padding – 15 pixels in this instance – to give breathing space. We do this in the same way that we added space to the #container layer.

Top: MSN makes good use of subtle graphical backgrounds, running faded images behind its sidebars and the main page

Bottom: Adding a faded graphical background to our #container layer focuses the reader's eye on the most important part of our page

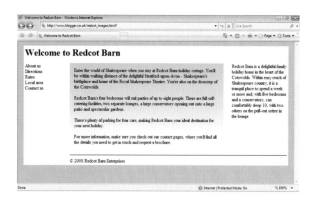

As you may have worked out, this introduces problems of its own. When we define the width of a layer (590 pixels in this instance), we are, in effect, defining the usable area. Adding 15 pixels to each side increases its overall width to 620 pixels. This is a disaster, as the overall layout no longer fits within the #container and the result is a mess. We can fix this by reducing the size of the #content layer by 30 pixels, trimming it from 590 to 560 to pull it back into line.

If you've been following this section on CSS closely, you may be able to work out for yourself how the #content styling must be amended. If not, here is the code we used:

```
#content {
    float: left;
    width: 560px;
    background-image: url(bgfade.gif);
    padding: 15px;
    background-repeat: repeat-x;
}
```

The image, which we named bgfade.gif and saved in the same folder as the page and stylesheet, is called in using `background-image`. This is very similar to the `background-color` code we used when applying a light green wash to the page as a whole, and the white background we added to the #container layer.

Creating a navigation bar

You now have all the tools needed to create an interactive navigation bar. Using CSS, plus the list tags in HTML, it's well within your grasp

Below: The default styling for an unordered list gives each entry a bullet point and arranges them all in a vertical column

In Chapter 3, we used the `<ol>` and `<ul>` tags to create lists of house rules for guests of Redcot Barn. However, confining these tags to mere list-making is a wasted opportunity, as they are the ideal starting point for creating CSS-styled menu bars. The tags already work in a hierarchical way, and each item in the list can be made to work as a little layer of its own, without the need to draw dozens of `<div>` tags.

List tags also provide an excellent example of the way browsers can skim over any commands they don't understand. This gives you a lot of freedom, as you can work on your designs safe in the knowledge that mistakes are unlikely to destroy your entire layout.

Once again, Internet Explorer diverges from the conventions used by almost every other browser in this area. As we saw when coding our three-column layout, only Internet Explorer is unable to centre our container layer when we split the redundant space on our page using the command `margins: auto;`. The same is true of the way it handles `:hover` states for anything

other than links; it doesn't handle them at all, at least not in IE7, the current version of the browser.

Over the next few pages, we'll create a menu that's compatible with all browsers, including IE7. We can then expand this to introduce a level of interactivity for other browsers that would previously have been possible only using Flash or a graphics application. We'll also show you where you can find the resources to emulate the same effects in Internet Explorer using third-party open-source code saved elsewhere on your site.

In this example, we'll return to the index.html and styles.css files we used in the previous project to add an interactive menu to pages. If you want to type in the code and try it for yourself, make sure you enter it exactly as it appears in the picture on page 68 and the basic HTML code on page 70.

ADDING THE MENU

First we need to add the menu entries to the index.html file. Open it in Notepad and add a new layer immediately below the header layer as follows:

```
<div id="widemenu"><ul><li>
<a href="">About us</a></li><li>
<a href="">Directions</a></li><li>
<a href="">Rates</a></li><li>
<a href="">Local area</a></li><li>
<a href="">Contact us</a></li></ul>
</div>
```

If you preview this in your browser, the menu appears as a bulleted list, because we've used the `<ul>` tag, denoting a list without ordinals (numbers). If we'd wanted to number each item on the list, we would have used an ordered list with the tag `<ol>`. For now we've also put empty links around every entry. We'll fill in their proper destinations later.

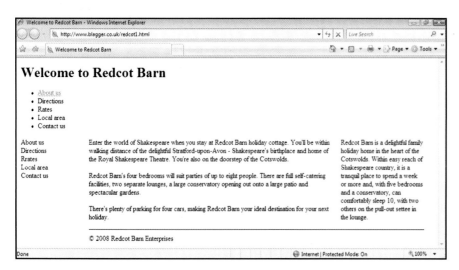

For now, the main problem with this menu is that it runs vertically and pushes all the remaining content of our page down. Save and close index.html and switch to styles.css, where we'll fix this as we start to style the menu to meet our needs.

Returning to a trick we used when creating a three-column layout, we'll arrange the menu entries side by side by floating them all to the left. As we discovered last time, if you float an item to the left and another item sits in its way, it will butt up against it. By floating every entry in the menu this way, we can easily get them to line up side by side in a single row. To achieve this, add the following section to styles.css, starting on a new line below the existing styles:

```
#widemenu ul li {
    float: left;
}
```

This compound class defines the target of our style very specifically. First, it tells the browser to confine the style data to elements found in the layer #widemenu. It then tells the browser to apply it only to list items (li) found in bulleted menus (ul). If we wanted to apply the style to items on any type of list in the #widemenu layer, we would leave out the ul section, and point lists with numbers would also adopt the style. If we wanted to apply it to all lists on our page, we'd leave out both the ul and #widemenu parts and open the tag with just li {.

Building up your targets in this way allows you to pinpoint precisely where you want your styles to apply, and define multiple styles for identical elements used in different parts of the page. If you wanted to use a different style for list items in an unordered list in the main content area of the page, for example, you would start with #content ul li {. The browser will know to differentiate between this and the styling for the menu.

BITING THE BULLET

If you now review index.html, you'll see that while we've sorted out the alignment, we've introduced another problem. The bullets are no longer appropriate and, apart from the first one, each bullet overlaps the end of the previous item in the menu. We'll solve this problem in two ways: first, by removing the bullets, and second, by defining the amount of space each list item takes up. The code to do this is added to the #widemenu ul li style:

```
#widemenu ul li {
    float: left;
    list-style-type: none;
    padding: 5px 30px 5px 5px;
}
```

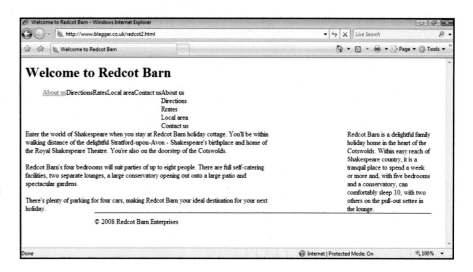

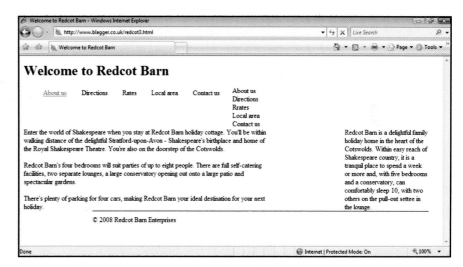

The list-style-type variable defines what should be used as the bullet for each entry in our list. Specifying none removes the bullet altogether. Alternatives include circle, square or a range of upper- and lower-case Roman numerals.

After removing the bullets, we also specified how the entries in the list should be padded, with five pixels of space above, below and to the left, and 30 pixels to the right of each. Alternatively, we could have specified a fixed width for the area each entry takes up – using width: 80px; for example. However, that would look uneven as longer entries such as 'Contact us' would fill their allotted area, while short ones such as 'Rates' would leave a lot of empty space.

Applying padding within each list item keeps them comfortably separate. When adding interactivity on those browsers that allow it, though, it also lets you simulate the effect of moving the mouse pointer over a large button that encompasses the entire area, not just the word itself.

We've almost finished working with the entries in our styled list, but there's one more task to complete. At the

Top: After removing the bullet and floating list items to the left, they line up side by side, but there's no space between them

Bottom: With some padding, the list items are nicely spaced out. Doing this rather than specifying a maximum area makes for a more comfortable effect. The left-most edge of each item may be a different distance from the left-hand edge of its predecessor, but the space between them, which is more obvious, is always equal

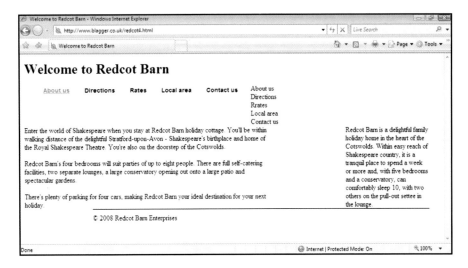

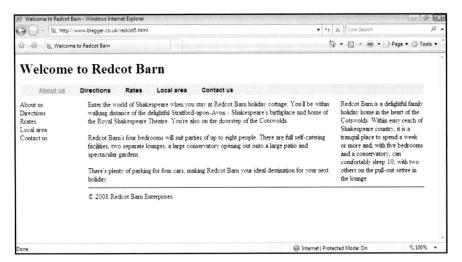

Then apply a dark red :hover state:

```
#widemenu ul li a:hover {
    color: #990000;
}
```

This looks better, but it's still not quite right. There's an obvious difference between the font used in the menu and the font used elsewhere on the page. Without clear limits around the menu, though, the two clash. Clearly the problem is no longer with the list itself, but rather the container in which it sits. As it's the same colour as the page, it's invisible. We could apply top and bottom borders, but that might be overkill, so instead we'll apply a light grey background (hexadecimal code DDDDDD) to pull the menu slightly forward from the rest of the page, and add a 10-pixel margin to the bottom to separate it from the rest of the content:

```
#widemenu {
    background-color: #dddddd;
    margin-bottom: 10px;
    height: 25px;
}
```

The page is looking better already, but our horizontal list is still inset too far for our liking. It should begin near the left-hand edge of the #widemenu layer. As it's bound by the <ul> and </ul> tags that define its left- and right-hand edges, we should now turn our attention to these to reposition the list as a whole, rather than the individual <li> elements we've been tweaking so far.

The reason the list is inset at the moment is that all lists in HTML are indented by default to make them easy to spot in a tract of running text, and to differentiate them from any numbers you might use to organise paragraphs or flowing text. We'll get rid of this indentation by changing both the margin and the padding of the <ul> tag used within the #widemenu layer to 0, like this:

```
#widemenu ul {
    margin: 0px;
    padding: 0px;
}
```

The menu now springs back towards the left-hand edge of the layer, aligning itself with the rest of the page.

APPLYING INTERACTIVITY

Our menu is now complete, but without links to other pages, and should render properly in any browser. However, as we've already said, it's easy to introduce visual feedback in any browser other than Internet Explorer through the judicious use of the :hover tag. Before version 7 you could do the same in Internet

Top: Now that our list items have their own style, they stand out from the page

Bottom: The underlying #widemenu layer now stretches across the width of the page with a grey background that clearly differentiates it from the rest of the page

moment, the list uses the same font as the rest of the page, which means it blends in a little too well. A menu should be differentiated so that a visitor can find it quickly, making it easier to navigate the site. Add three lines between the padding: 5px 30px 5px 5px; and the closing } of the #widemenu ul li section:

```
font-family: Arial, Helvetica,
 sans-serif;
font-weight: bold;
font-size: 14px;
```

To remove the colours and underlines from the links so that they look more like part of the menu bar and less like plain links, we'll target links (a) within list items (li) within bulleted lists (ul) in the #widemenu area:

```
#widemenu ul li a {
    color: #000000;
    text-decoration: none;
}
```

Explorer using the same commands, but now it only accepts :hover when added to the <a> link tag.

For the moment, we'll concentrate on those browsers that are compatible and apply the :hover class to <li> tags that define the entries in our menu list. We've already shown how to apply a :hover state to a link (page 68). CSS styles attached to an element remain active in any variation of that element unless you definitively overrule them, so we don't need to rewrite the code for the li style from scratch. Instead, we can allow the hovered-over element to retain its existing styling, and add a new style point that only ever comes into play when the mouse is over each element, using this code:

```
#widemenu ul li:hover {
    background-color: #BBBBBB;
}
```

Save styles.css and open index.html in any browser other than IE to see what effect this has on your page. Roll your mouse backwards and forwards along the menu line, and you'll see that every time you pass over an item in the menu its background gets darker. This background extends across the width we defined for the invisible box, which contains each entry in the menu.

To achieve such an effect before CSS, you'd have had to create two buttons for each entry in the menu: one that displays when the mouse is away from the menu, and one that appears as the mouse passes over it. This eats into your bandwidth and is needlessly complicated to code.

Potentially more serious, however, is the fact that if you were to change the structure of your site later and you needed to alter the menu to reflect this, you would have to re-create your buttons from scratch in your graphics application. Using the CSS approach outlined here, you can do the same thing with nothing more sophisticated than the copy of Notepad that's built into Windows.

You don't need to make any changes to achieve the same effect in Internet Explorer, but you do need to take advantage of its handling of 'behaviours' for onscreen elements. These are defined in separate files, which you include in your page as part of your stylesheet, and which in effect rewrite some of the browser's internal workings. One such behaviour rewrites every :hover state found on your page so that it acts as a JavaScript mouseover command. This is still a commonly used means of introducing more complex interactivity into your pages. You can download this behaviour from http://tinyurl.com/csshover, after which you copy and paste it into a new file and save it into the root of your site as csshover.htc.

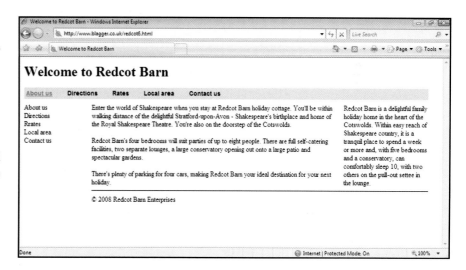

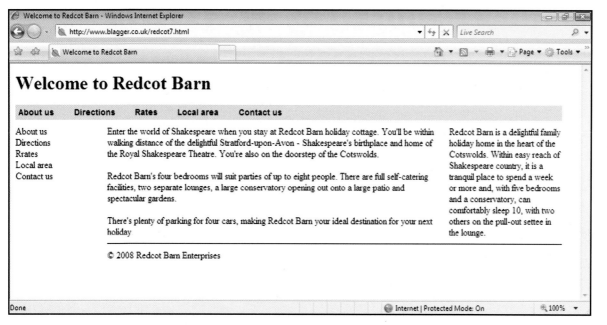

Above: After changing the padding and margin values to 0, the menu entries have the same left-hand margin as the text on the page

Left: Finally, we address the styling of the links in the menu by removing the text decoration and changing the colour to black, making the active elements look like proper entries on a menu bar

Looking good

You've made sure your pages are packed with content that visitors will want to read, and you've checked that your website is well coded and will work on any browser. However, it's crucial that it looks good, too.

Even if you're not a professional designer, you can still take steps to ensure that your website meets the highest possible standards. Simply take some cues from those sites you consider particularly attractive, user-friendly and easy to read.In this chapter, we'll explore the lessons to be learned from successful websites such as the BBC's. You'll discover the benefits of optimising and saving images for the web so pages load quickly. We'll also take a closer look at typography and graphic design, and tell you which rules to follow — and which you can break.

Finding inspiration

Successful, dynamic websites have been created by professionals, so you shouldn't be afraid to borrow the best bits from your favourites

Below left: By using two horizontal menu bars in concert, you give visitors immediate access to major sections while providing a link to pages in the current section, as on the Guardian and Independent websites

Below right: The BBC employs a vertical menu and embeds sub-sections within the main category flow

The main elements of a web page can be put together in many different ways, but there are some things to remember. Your menu can go above, to the left or right of your content, but you shouldn't put links only at the bottom. While your web address will always appear in the browser's location bar, you should replicate the name near the top of the page. Finally, you shouldn't put your most important content so far down the page that you have to scroll to see it. These are all things we touched on in Chapter 2 when we were planning our website.

The best way to gauge how a well-designed website works is to look at some of the web's biggest names. The BBC's online presence covers everything from Radio 4's schedules to videos from CBeebies, taking in weather, sport and user chat. Yet it has a uniform style and matching positions for common elements on each page. Load your favourite BBC page via www.bbc.co.uk and

you'll see how, wherever you are, the BBC logo is in the top-left corner, always linking back to the front page. Now visit www.microsoft.com, www.cnn.com and www. youtube.com and you'll see that they all do the same. Google's homepage is slightly different, as it's famed for sitting its iconic brand in the centre of the page above a single search box. However, when you get to the results pages, it obediently shuffles back to the top left corner.

These sites all do this because years of web use have conditioned us to expect a link back to the homepage in that position, or at least in close proximity.

MENU MASTERS

How you structure the rest of your links is up to you. However, as a general rule you should start your menu (navigation bar) immediately below the homepage link, running horizontally, vertically, or in both directions at once. These horizontal and vertical menus can duplicate

each other, but it is often better to split them. Use one for linking major sections of your site, and one to handle pages within those sections. Alternatively, run the menus side by side, but make one subservient to the other.

Take a look at the menus on three of the UK's most-visited newspaper websites: www.independent.co.uk, www.guardian.co.uk and www.timesonline.co.uk. See how each website has a main menu below the logo area linking to the various parts of the site, with a submenu running below the main menu that divides each major section into its constituent parts.

If you're going to use vertical menus, you can go further and integrate the submenu with the main sections through careful use of differing font weights and background colours. Visit http://news.bbc.co.uk and click World in the left-hand margin to see how the menu opens up to display a world map and section names that break up the globe roughly by continent.

Whether horizontal or vertical, these menu systems do one thing very well: they keep links to every main section of the site – the homepage and the primary subject areas – visible at all times. This helps their visitors to understand how the content they are reading fits into the bigger picture, and lets them navigate the site more quickly. They don't have to back-track through all their recently viewed pages to an appropriate junction that will enable them to head off in another direction; in every example, they can go from an obscure sports story to the latest finance news in no more than two clicks.

HOLD THE FRONT PAGE

Most of the biggest sites structure their homepages like a list of departments in a high street store. They never try to cram everything into the first page, but instead pick out a few key stories and link on to the rest.

The UK's government portal at http://direct.gov.uk has so much to cram in that its designers cannot hope to guess whether you're looking for statistics on the likely incidence of a flu pandemic or details about local paper recycling. Instead, the front page is a collection of links organised into a logical hierarchy, with some key stories arranged to the right in a box marked 'In the news'.

It is unlikely that your own site will grow to this size, but you can certainly draw inspiration from the way that its administrators have made editorial decisions and hand-picked a small range of the most compelling content. Think about the focus of your site and put that right on your front page, relegating less important details to other parts of your site.

If we consider our holiday home example, the most important details are the location and the facilities that might tempt a visitor to book a week's stay. Contact details and directions can be demoted to linked pages along with prices, which we don't want visitors to see until the front page description has done its job and convinced them to book.

Above: Three leading sites with one thing in common: all include a link in the top left-hand corner that takes you back to the homepage

Even the big players use this philosophy for their front pages; www.hilton.co.uk highlights new openings and events, www.harvester.co.uk promotes new items on its menu and www.apple.com showcases new technology. Each gives just a hint of the content found elsewhere, leaving the visitor free to explore at their own pace.

STRIKING A BALANCE

Although it's helpful to refer to popular websites for your site, you need to keep things in perspective. Carbon-copying another site won't work for your content. Each page on your site carries elements that are common to every other page on your own site, and uniquely tailored to best present the information you have to offer; it's unlikely anyone else's designs could present your content better than you can. Keep in mind the importance of clear, well-structured links that let you present just enough content on each page and encourage your visitors to explore elsewhere without leaving your site altogether.

Left: The UK government portal is so wide-ranging, the site editors have presented the homepage as a sectionalised directory, with highlighted features in a strip at the top and the In The News box lower right

Working with images

As well as knowing which images are right for your website, you need to understand compression, cropping, sharpening and watermarking

BENEFITS ●●●

- Optimise photos for fast page-loading times
- Find the right balance between file size and quality
- Protect your images from theft by using watermarks

We touched briefly on working with images on page 54. Because they are the most data-intensive elements on a page, they'll consume your bandwidth and disk space more voraciously than anything else on your site. Therefore, it's essential that you compress your images before uploading them to your site, both to ensure they download quickly and to avoid exceeding any limits on your hosting account.

SAVING GRACES

The first step in saving your images for online use is to understand how they will be used. Photos should be saved in JPEG format, since compression tools can merge areas of similar colour. Flat graphics, such as logos with solid colours, should be saved in GIF or PNG format, from which compression tools will remove colours and use dithering to fool the eye into thinking they are still there.

Most graphics applications will have a dedicated web-saving mode, giving you a preview of the results of your compression. It's essential that you use this rather than just using a Save As option from the File menu, as heavy compression can have a detrimental effect on your finished page unless it is handled carefully.

As a general rule the more complex an image is, the less it can be compressed. The two right-hand images below are sections of a JPEG, which we ran through Photoshop's Save for Web feature with quality settings of 0 per cent and 100 per cent. While the image at 0 per cent quality (middle) will download quickly, a close look reveals artefacts and blocking, which will make your site look tatty and unprofessional. The image saved at 100 per cent (right) looks great, but will take a long time to download. Setting the quality to 50 per cent is the best compromise in most cases.

Likewise, the three images on the page opposite show a graphic saved in GIF format with eight, 32 and 256 colours. Because we have applied dithering, there's little difference between the 32- and 256-colour versions, yet the file size is smaller: 92KB as opposed to 144KB. Clearly, then, the most appropriate compression in this instance is to reduce the number of colours to 32 and

Below: JPEG is a highly efficient compression method. When the photo below is examined up close, you can see the compression in action. The one in the middle has been heavily compressed and the one on the right lightly compressed

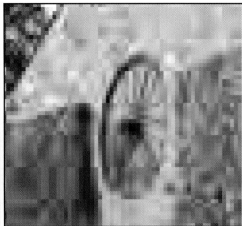

8 colours

32 colours

256 colours

apply dithering. The eight-colour image, though, looks awful and the subtle graduated fade to the sky is no longer smooth, but stepped, and thus unusable.

CLEAR AND SIMPLE

Images used on the web are usually published in a physically smaller format than they ever would be for printing, and are rarely more than 500 pixels in width when embedded in text. Images that are used to illustrate an article or story (rather than being the main focus, as they are in Flickr galleries) are often even smaller still, and should be cropped in a graphics application before being used on the page.

Smaller graphics can be harder to see clearly, and so increasing saturation and sharpening in Photoshop can pay dividends. Use the Unsharp Mask filter via Filter, Sharpen, Unsharp Mask. Start with the amount set to 40%, the radius to 1.5 pixels and the threshold 2. Make sure the Preview option is ticked so you can see the results of your selections, then adjust the pixels slider until you achieve the desired result. You're looking for high-contrast edges to stand out without degrading areas of solid colour around them.

When working with monochrome images, the High Pass filter is often a better choice, but it shouldn't be applied to your original image, as this will make things worse. Instead, duplicate your small image on to a new layer sitting above the original. With this new layer active, select the High Pass filter using Filter, Other, High Pass. Set the radius to 5 pixels and click OK. The result will look terrible and give you an idea of what you would have achieved if you hadn't duplicated the layer.

Now return to the Layers palette. With the newly created layer still selected, use the drop-down menu at the top of the palette to change the blending mode to Hard Light. This uses the High Pass layer to increase the contrast in the original monochrome image, giving very strong blacks and whites. If the effect is too strong for your needs, you can tailor it precisely by decreasing the High Pass layer's visibility using the Opacity input box to

the right of the Blend Mode drop-down. When you're happy with the result, amalgamate the layers of your image by selecting Layer, Flatten Image, and save it for web use. Don't save over your original image. Images that are sharpened often don't compress as well as those that aren't, so you may have to use less ambitious compression settings so as not to spoil the results.

MAKE YOUR MARK

Putting your images online makes them susceptible to theft. Although you can make them trickier to steal, there's not much you can do to make them theft-proof. The best you can hope for is to make them less desirable, while not spoiling them for genuine visitors. Photoshop and other graphics applications let you watermark your work so it is identifiable if it turns up on another site.

To apply a simple watermark, create a new layer that sits on top of your image. Type a line of text, in white, identifying yourself and the site where the image is to be used. Change the layer's blending mode to Soft Light. The text becomes semi-transparent, allowing you to see the image through it while branding it as your own.

Carefully position the watermark so it sits over an important yet difficult-to-edit part of your image, which cannot easily be cloned out, then save the results for use on your site. Again, don't save over your original image. To find out more about what you can do with images for your website, see Chapters 7 and 9.

Above: Reducing the number of colours in the image to eight degrades the left-hand image. The remaining images are almost impossible to tell apart, but the one on the right is over 50KB larger than the one in the middle, which has only 32 colours and 100 per cent compression. The image on the right has 256 colours and 100 per cent compression

Below: Using a high-pass filter increases the contrast in this monochrome image (left) so it has more impact and is clearer at small sizes (right)

Good graphic design

You know how to put your website together, but remembering our rules about typography and page layout will ensure that it really stands out

Below: The Guardian uses just two fonts: a serif font in its headlines and menus, and a sans serif font for body copy

It's easy to think of the graphic design of your site as relating only to the actual images used on a page. However, it actually encompasses the design of the entire page, including its layout and colours and, in its most expansive sense, it should also include the physical structure and the typesetting of your text – a graphical discipline known as typography.

FONT OF KNOWLEDGE
You may have 100 fonts on your computer, but that's no reason to use them all. Indeed, the fewer you use the better. On page 34, we mentioned the benefit of limiting your choice, but this particular point is worth reiterating. Look at some of your most-visited sites, and news sites in particular, and you'll see that there are just one or two

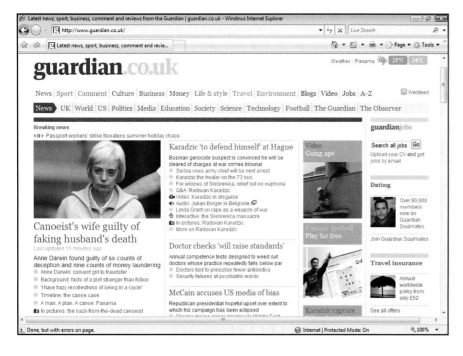

fonts used on the page. The designers will have used different weights (normal and bold) and introduced typographical elements such as bulleted lists and pullquotes to differentiate sections of the text and move your eye from one point to the next.

If you choose two fonts, make a series of rules about how and where each should be used, and stick to them on every page of your website. One should be a body copy font, which is easy to read at small sizes, and the other should be used for headings. Menus are often best rendered using a larger, heavier weight of your body font. Make sure your two fonts contrast dramatically. The easiest way to do this is to choose one sans serif family, such as 'Arial, Helvetica, sans serif', and one serif family, such as 'Georgia, Times New Roman, Times'. It was once said that you should use the sans serif font for your headlines and the serif font for your body copy, as is common in print design, but web design is defining a style of its own and, with the arrival of sites such as WordPress and Twitter, large serif fonts are becoming increasingly common in headlines.

Likewise, we are seeing less frequent use of Verdana, a font designed specifically for easy onscreen legibility; it was distributed by Microsoft as part of Windows and Office (on the PC and Mac) and through its website. It was very common on websites in the 1990s and, as a result, it can make a site that uses it look rather dated.

INNER SPACE
Another typographical consideration is the spacing between your lines. A common misconception among first-time designers is that by making your characters large you are making your words more legible, but in many cases this can actually have the opposite effect.

Instead, you should leave the characters the same size and instead increase the line spacing using the CSS command `line-height` to be one and a half times your font size in pixels (we show you how to do this in Chapter 4). This loosens up your whole layout and helps your visitor's eye to scan each line quickly and easily. This is particularly important where you are running comparatively long lines of text across the screen, which can be hard to track from one end to the other.

SHADY BUSINESS

You should approach colour selection in a similar way to fonts and avoid saturating your pages with a broad spectrum of colours. We touched on this on page 37. Choose a colour palette that represents your subject – for example, greens for a garden centre or holidays in the country, blues for beach holidays, reds for businesses and so on – and use variations throughout your site. Use three distinct tones for various areas: a lighter tone with an opacity of 20 per cent or less for solid backgrounds; a darker tone for headlines, crossheads and section labels; and a mid-tone for highlights such as hover-over areas on menus or links in your text. Refer to page 38 to find out how to use Adobe Kuler to make a selection.

Some colour combinations don't work well and are uncomfortable on the eye, such as yellow on red, or red on blue; such combinations can make reading difficult. Others combinations will cause problems for visitors with a visual impairment, as we explained on page 41. Red/green colour-blindness, for example, is common. As such, you should avoid using combinations of these colours with similar levels of brightness or opacity, when it's essential that they are easily distinguishable from each other – for example, when colouring a list of good and bad foods on a diet plan. If you must use them, ensure that they are accompanied by another hinting device such as clear headings.

For the same reason, you should always make sure that your text and background colours are distinct from each other. You may find dark blue text on a light blue background, grey on white or orange on yellow perfectly readable, but you are probably in the minority. Furthermore, you have no way of knowing whether the colour calibration on your visitors' monitors matches your own. As such, you should avoid using different strengths of the same colour on top of one another. Remember, there is a very good reason why most newspapers, magazines, books and websites use plain black text on white: it works.

STAND IN LINE

No matter how faithfully you follow this advice, it can all be undone if the underlying structure of your page layout is weak. On page 70, we showed you how to create a very simple three-column layout, where every margin was 10 pixels wide, whether between the vertical columns or length-wise between the horizontal menu and the start of the content. Ten pixels should be common throughout. When we styled the footer, we

pushed it 160 pixels in from the left-hand edge so it lined up with the start of the main content area. That edge is then a common theme on the page because it is shared by two layers.

Strong web designs work because they are instantly familiar. A small collection of fonts, a narrow range of harmonious colours and a layout where each element lines up will let your visitor quickly scan the page to get to the information they want, bypassing the menus and headers they don't need straightaway. The result is a more professional finish, and yet another reason for visitors to keep returning to your site.

Top: The BBC's underlying grid is strong, with matching horizontal and vertical margins between each section

Above: Increased line spacing, as at WordPress.org, often improves the legibility of your text more effectively than increased font size can

Content management

A content management system, or CMS for short, is a convenient way of managing lots of web pages. You determine the content, such as a diary entry, and the 'system' manages the way posts are shown and provides you with a way to create new posts.

In this chapter, we'll explain how to integrate a blog into your website using WordPress. A blog is an example of a simple CMS, but if you're building a large website you won't want to create every page by hand and will need a more advanced CMS such as Joomla, which we look at here. Both WordPress and Joomla need a database for storing the content, which your web host should provide. Fortunately, Joomla and WordPress are both free, so it won't cost you anything to use them.

Writing a blog

A blog is a terrific way to voice an opinion on an informal website or consolidate an identity on a professional site, and it's easy to add one

- Find out how to get a blog on your website
- Keep visitors up to date
- Give people a reason to come back to your site

The word blog comes from the longer phrase 'web log'. Put simply, a blog is like an online diary. In the past five years, blogs have become incredibly popular. Technorati (www.technorati.com) is a service that tracks blogs, and it is currently monitoring over 112 million of them – that's two for every person in the UK. There are blogs for every subject imaginable. Politicians (www.webcameron.org.uk), musicians (www.charlottechurch.com) and actors (www.stephenfry.com)

have ventured into blogging. With minimal effort, you can, too. You never know, it might even help your business.

SINGLE SERVING

A blog distinguishes itself from a news site through its design. Most blogs are presented on a single page with each entry sitting above the preceding one, so it's easy for people to keep track of what you're writing about.

Right: Blogger is one of the most popular free blogging applications around

A blog is tremendously flexible by its nature. You can use one to chronicle anything of a witty or trivial nature; www.wifeinthenorth.com, for example, details "one woman's journey into the northern heartlands". At its most focused, however, a blog can be an effective way to raise awareness about a cause or charity, or to keep people informed about upcoming events.

Blogs are primarily text, with a few pictures sprinkled here and there. However, as long as entries appear on your site in reverse chronological order, it's a blog. As such, you could record your entries on a video camera (this is called vlogging), or you could use just pictures (photoblogging) or recorded sound (podcasting).

Individual entries don't have to be long, so you need to write only a few dozen words every day for your website to look fresh and updated whenever people visit.

INSTANT GRATIFICATION

The popularity of blogging is proven by the number of blogs on the internet, and the number of people who read them. Perez Hilton (www.perezhilton.com), a foul-mouthed, celebrity-focused blog, attracts an estimated three million readers per month.

Part of the reason for the popularity of blogs is that they offer a quick hit of information. Whether you write a few lines a day or a few hundred words a week, people will be happy to read your blog, as it will take them only a few minutes to catch up with your comings and goings.

A blog makes even more sense if you can round up a few fans. If you sell your photos, for instance, you'll find that the people who buy them will be interested in seeing how and when you take your pictures. Alternatively, you could make a name for yourself if you're an entertaining writer or someone with out-of-the-ordinary opinions.

Another reason blogging is popular is that it's so easy. Setting up an e-commerce website (see page 116) or

designing navigation elements (see page 76) are involved processes, even with the benefit of time-saving measures such as CSS. Most blogging software, by comparison, takes under an hour to set up. Creating entries or customising the appearance of your blog couldn't be simpler. A blog takes little (and in some cases, no) technical knowledge to set up, yet is accessible by anyone with an internet connection.

Finally, most blogs act as gateways. It's standard blogging practice to have links to other blogs in a list known as a blogroll. If you find a blog you like, it's likely there'll be a list of other, similar blogs on the same page. It is possible to spend hours browsing these blogs, and you stand a very good chance of stumbling across something you'll return to again and again.

CASH IN HAND

It's unlikely that you'll get rich by writing a blog, although it has happened to a few people. Still, you may be able to make money if you host adverts on your blog. You can do this with Google's AdSense program (see page 116 for details). However, you'll need a large number of readers before you make any real money.

Another way of turning your blog into gold is to set your sights on getting published. Using the nom de plume of Belle De Jour, a London call girl wrote a saucy blog about her exploits, which was then turned into a best-selling book called *The Intimate Adventures of a London Call Girl* (Phoenix Publishing). It later became a TV series. Again, bear in mind that the chances of your blog making it from screen to print are small.

The best way to turn your blog into something commercially viable is to tie it in with your business. Commercial blogging – where the blog is hosted by a company and is primarily about its day-to-day business – is taking off in a big way. Companies that have blogs

Blogs are your chance to share your thoughts on all manner of subjects, whether you happen to be a witty wordsmith such as Stephen Fry (left) or a candid chanteuse such as Charlotte Church (right)

Top left: Even politicians such as David Cameron are sampling the delights of blogging; see www.webcameron.org.uk for details

Top right: WordPress is a free control management system that you install on your web space

Below: The experiences of a wife and mother who has relocated to Northumberland are chronicled at www. wifeinthenorth.com

can push their corporate philosophy on to readers in the hope of turning them into customers. Blogs also make businesses seem more personable.

A corporate blog allows people to listen in on your daily business and keep track of interesting-sounding projects. For example, Microsoft has around 700 employees who actively blog. Consequently, customers and fans know about key projects without having to wait for them to be covered in the mainstream media.

It's worth remembering that a blog has the potential to reach anyone who is online. There's a chance someone will stumble across your blog one day – an impossibility if your only electronic outreach is via a giant email list.

ALL SYSTEMS GO

Starting up your own blog is incredibly easy. There are two main ways to do this: you can either sign up for a

free account with a service that will give you some web space and a content management system (CMS) for making posts, or you can integrate blogging software into your existing website.

One of the most popular free blogging applications is Blogger, which is owned by Google. Signing up is straightforward: if you already have a Google account (which you will, if you use Gmail or any of Google's other online offerings) then half the work is done for you. Simply choose a username and the name of your blog, and you're away.

There are plenty of ways to customise it; there are dozens of templates, as well as the ability to select your own colour scheme. This gives plenty of scope for looking different to other blogs.

Signing up to Blogger makes you part of a blogging community: it's a good way to find like-minded bloggers. Best of all, because it is a hosted blog, there's no coding, no need to grapple with FTP servers, and no associated costs. It's a great way to start out with your first blog.

FREEDOM OF THE PRESS

If you already have a website, it doesn't make sense to use a hosted blogging service: you're already paying for web space, so why get more? In this case, a service such as WordPress is ideal. WordPress is a free CMS that you download to your web space. You'll see how to do this on the page opposite.

WordPress's great strength – apart from the fact that it's free and can be hosted on any web space – is that it's massively customisable. You can download a huge number of themes, and even create your own to match the look of your website, if you're technically minded. Alternatively, if you fancy investing in your blog, you can buy themes from professional designers.

You can also change the way that your blog works with the help of plug-ins (see Step 5, opposite); again, the more ambitious can write their own. This means your blog will look unique, and you'll be able to build in features as you need them.

How to... Set up WordPress

1 Go to www.wordpress.org. Download the latest version of the software. Log in to your website's FTP server using the details supplied by your hosting provider and copy across the contents of the WordPress folder. Your web host needs to support PHP and at least one MySQL database. See page 12 for a table comparing hosting packages.

2 Set up a MySQL database using your website's 'back end'. Check with your web host if you're unsure how to do this. Edit the wp-config.php file on your web space to reflect the details of your database. If you need more help you'll find support forums on WordPress's website, where you can get help from more experienced users.

3 In your browser, visit your website but add /wp-admin to the address. You'll be presented with a login screen, where you'll need to choose a password. After this, you'll find yourself at the Dashboard, which you'll use to write posts and change the way your blog looks and works.

4 Click on Design. By default, WordPress comes with a few templates built in, but there are hundreds more at http://themes. wordpress.net. Here, you can sort themes by the number of columns they have or the colours they use, or by keyword.

Once you've chosen a theme and downloaded it, copy it into your wp-content/ themes folder on your web space. It will appear in the Themes section of the WordPress Dashboard. Clicking on a theme will bring up a preview showing you what the theme looks like with your content in place, before you activate it. Here you can also apply the HTML and CSS you learned in Chapters 3 and 4. WordPress themes are simply PHP files with a CSS file dictating their style. You can experiment with the CSS file to get your blog looking just the way you want it.

5 To get your blog working flawlessly, you'll need a few plug-ins. A plug-in is a tiny application that works with a piece of software to provide a new function. In WordPress, this could be gathering statistics, playing videos or running a slideshow. There are thousands of plug-ins available, with plentiful community support. Just go to http://plugins.wordpress.net and search around for something you like.

6 With your blog set up, remember the basics: always link to external sources of information, add new posts frequently and make sure you link to a few other interesting blogs to keep people coming back. Adhere to these rules, and your readership will grow.

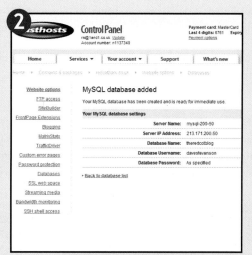

Using a content management system

If you have a large website, a content-management system such as the free Joomla can help to coordinate the efforts of multiple contributors

Below: Joomla is one of the most popular open-source content management systems

When a website reaches a certain size, or if more than a couple of people need to work on content at once, then working directly with HTML files on a web server and managing links between pages by hand can become unwieldy. This is where a content management system (CMS) comes in handy.

A CMS is a database-driven website. Content is created using a text editor in an administrative area of the site (known as the 'back-end'), where it's broken down into constituent parts (such as the creator's name, the title, the main content, images and so on) before being stored in a database on the web server. The CMS then extracts the content from the database and publishes it as a complete web page on the site, or 'front-end'.

The main advantage of using a CMS-based website is that, being database-driven, it enables one person to manage content created by lots of different people. Since content and layout information are stored separately, a CMS-based site adheres to the principles that we talked about in Chapters 3 and 4. Therefore, the design of a site can be changed without having to worry about how the content will fit into it, and the site can be successfully viewed in a variety of browsers on a range of devices.

Since content is generated dynamically (it doesn't exist as a web page stored on the server, but is created by the CMS on demand), a CMS-based website makes efficient use of server space. Even very large sites can be contained in just a few megabytes.

OPEN FOR BUSINESS

There are several commercial content management systems (Blogger is one), but some of the best are open-source applications. In addition to being free to download and use, an open-source CMS can be freely modified. This means it can be fine-tuned to meet most requirements. Sadly, open-source software can be buggy and often lacks good documentation. Still, the open-source community is usually very helpful when it comes to fixing problems and providing technical support.

One of the most popular open-source content management systems is Joomla. Currently at version 1.5, Joomla is a spin-off of another open-source CMS called Mambo, which started life in 2000, so its heritage is a good deal greater than its version number might suggest.

You can download Joomla free from www.joomla.org. Joomla 1.0 is available, but its development has ceased, so it is recommended only if you need to use a template or extension that isn't compatible with Joomla 1.5.

If you want to try Joomla without installing it on your web server, there's a demo installation available at http://demo.joomla.org. Once you've registered with a valid email address, you can log into the administrative back-end of a standard Joomla installation to get a feel

How to... Install Joomla

1 Upload the Joomla files to your web server using an FTP program. You may be able to upload the compressed .zip, .tar.gz or .tar.bz2 file and decompress it on the server. If not, you'll have to extract the file on your computer and upload the resulting assortment of files and folders.

2 Once the files and folders have transferred, you can use your web browser to go to the root of your Joomla folder on your web server; this is usually just the root folder, or a URL such as www. redcotbarn.co.uk. You should see the first page of Joomla's online setup process. If not, check that you're looking in the correct folder, and that all the files have completely unzipped or uploaded.

3 The installation process is largely self-explanatory. It will check that your web server is properly configured to support a Joomla installation. If any tests under 'Pre-installation Check' are marked as No, you must check your web server's settings or contact your hosting provider.

4 Mid-way through the Joomla installation, you'll need to provide a hostname, database name, username and password for the database you're going to use. The hostname is usually 'localhost'; the other settings are those you noted when you created the database with your web host prior to installing Joomla.

5 You'll be prompted for a website name, along with an email address and an administrator password at the end of the installation. You'll also have the chance to install some sample data, so Joomla isn't a blank slate when you start. It's also worth clicking the Install Sample Data button to get you started; you can always delete this data afterwards.

6 Before you can use Joomla, you need to delete the entire Installation folder from the FTP server; you should see a message to this effect. You can then click the Site or Admin buttons to see the site's front-end or back-end.

REQUIREMENTS
Joomla requires a web server that supports PHP, MySQL and Apache. MySQL, XML and Zlib need to be enabled in the PHP installation.

Ask your web-hosting company if it supports Joomla; if it does, it will have everything you need. Even if your hosting package doesn't include a MySQL database, it may be possible to add one for an annual fee.

for things. Alternatively, you can use a free Apache distribution such as XAMPP from www.apachefriends. org/en/xampp.html to create a web server on your PC. This lets you install and use Joomla on your computer.

You can download Joomla 1.5 from http://tinyurl. com/downloadjoomla. The Zip, Tar.gz and Tar.bz2 files are 6MB, 4MB and 3MB respectively. For Windows you'll want the Zip file, while the others are for Linux-based hosts.

Before you start the Joomla installation, you'll need to create a database on your web server. This is done via the administrator control panel for your web server or through the phpMyAdmin utility; check with your web hosting provider if you're not sure. Once the database is created, make a note of its name and the username and password of the account that has access to it.

MAKING JOOMLA WORK FOR YOU

A fresh installation of Joomla has enough features to create a pretty sophisticated website. If you chose to install the sample data in 'How to… Install Joomla' on page 95 your site will already look like it's fully functioning. You will, of course, want to change the sample data to something that you've created yourself, and you'll probably also want to change the design of the site. However, you'll need to know a little about how a Joomla-based site works before attempting this.

Log into the Joomla administrative panel (the 'back-end') from www.yoursitename.com/administrator. The default username is admin and the password is the one that you entered in Step 5 of 'How to… Install Joomla'. The first thing you'll see when you log in is the Control Panel with buttons for several key administrative tasks.

Joomla organises its content, called 'articles', into one or more sections and optional subsections, called categories. Articles from any section or category can be automatically displayed on the site's homepage, or 'front page', as well as displayed on their own individual section or category pages. Think of it like a newspaper, where

How to... Add an article

1 Sections and categories are created and managed from the Content menu. You must create a section before you can create categories within it; the sample data installed as part of the walkthrough on page 95 includes a selection of both.

2 Articles are added via the Add New article button on the Control Panel or Content, Article Manager, New. An article has several components. Title is the name of the article that appears on the front-end. Alias is an optional longer title used for search engine optimisation (SEO); see page 122 for details of a project dealing with this. You can write the content for your article in the WYSWYG editor.

All articles have an option for Published or Front Page. Published controls whether or not an article is visible on the site, whereas Front Page controls whether it's visible on the front page.

3 Click Image at the bottom of the WYSIWYG editor pane to add an image to an article. An image browser appears. Either choose an image already stored on the web server or click the Browse button to select and upload one from your PC.

4 The Article Manager lets you see all content on your site. Use the drop-down menus to filter it by Section, Category or Author. Change the state of an article by clicking the icons in the Published and Front Page columns, or make changes across the board by ticking the appropriate articles and using the buttons that run across the top of this page.

5 Go to Extensions, Module Manager to assign Joomla components to parts of your template. The main screen shows a list and the state of the currently installed modules. Click any module and

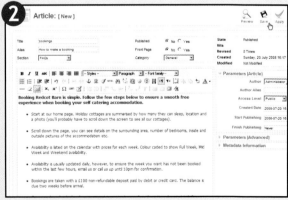

the front page contains stories pulled from the different sections (politics, entertainment, sport and so on) inside.

You'll need to map out the sections and categories that you want to use for your website before you start adding content. Still, you can create new sections and categories, delete old ones and move articles around at any time, so any plans you make aren't permanent.

EYE FOR DESIGN

Joomla is a template-based content management system, which means that the design of a Joomla-based site is governed by one or more layout files stored separately to the content. The layout can be altered by changing the template, as long as the new design takes into account the content, so that there's sufficient room for images in columns of text, the site logo is in the appropriate place and so on.

A Joomla template can be as simple as an HTML file with tables that control the position of page elements, or it can consist of a series of sophisticated CSS-based designs that create a different design for each page. Fortunately, you don't need any programming or design skills to make a slick Joomla site; there are dozens of sites that have great-looking free and low-cost commercial templates for download (see the box below).

GETTING INTO POSITION

Joomla uses the idea of 'modules' to publish content on a page. A template has a number of module positions. The positions to which you assign different types of content govern the overall look of your site.

For example, your site might contain an ad, a photo gallery, a list of menus and some legal fine print, along with your main content. The ad might be best placed in the 'banner' position that runs across the top of the page, with the menu in the column that runs down the left-hand side. The bulk of your content is usually displayed down the middle of the page, and you can specify how many columns it occupies and whether to display the whole article or just an excerpt that links to the full page.

you will be able to change its module position and other parameters.

6 You can go to Extensions, Template Manager to manage installed site templates (however, template editing is best done in a separate external HTML editor). Upload a template from Extensions, Install/Uninstall, Templates. Templates are usually downloaded as compressed files; you can upload these directly without having to decompress them.

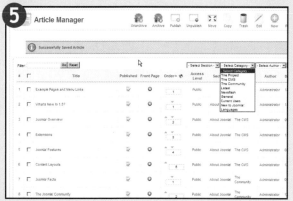

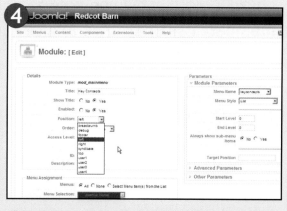

JOOMLA RESOURCES

• http://extensions. joomla.org
Hundreds of free and commercial add-ons for Joomla that cater for every conceivable site requirement.

• http://forum. joomla.org
The official Joomla support forum; the first port of call for any Joomla questions or technical support requests.

• www.rocket theme.com
• www.gavick.com
• www.joomla shack.com
Three excellent Joomla template providers, offering a mix of free and low-cost, high-quality templates.

Adding sparkle

By now, you should be more confident about creating a good-looking website that your visitors can navigate easily. You're now in a position to go a step further and make your website really special by adding a few flourishes here and there.

In this chapter, we'll show you how to add video, panoramic images, slideshows, weather forecasts and even driving directions to your pages. If you know that you're going to be updating your website frequently, you'll also benefit from creating an RSS feed to let people know when there's something new to read. Finally, if you're setting up a website for a club or church, we'll show you how to add a forum so that members can chat, give advice, arrange meetings and more besides.

YouTube video

A video can give your website added appeal and bring a page to life in minutes. Here we show you how to turn those thoughts into action

ESSENTIALS ●●●

SKILL LEVEL
Beginner
Intermediate
Expert

HOW LONG
30 minutes

s recently as 2006, hosting a video on a website was a complicated matter. Thankfully, this has changed. Adding a video clip to your site can be done in a few minutes, and all for free. Here we show you how to add a YouTube video to your site.

1 Prepare your video for uploading. YouTube accepts videos in a range of formats, including AVI, MPG and MOV. For the best results, use an MPEG4 format such as DivX or XviD. A free video encoder such as Any Video Converter (www.any-video-converter.com) will change your video to one of these formats. Select 640x480 as the resolution; this will give the best quality because of the way YouTube compresses files. Clips can't be longer than 10 minutes, and are limited to 1GB.

2 To upload your clip, you need a YouTube account. If you don't have one, sign up for free at www.youtube.com. Once you're registered, click on the yellow Upload button on the right-hand side. You must add a title, description and tags, but go to town with these only if you want YouTube users to find your video easily. Click the 'Upload a video…' button and select the file. Uploading takes a while, since your broadband connection's upload speed is likely to be much slower than the download speed. For this reason, we recommend limiting your video's file size to 20MB.

3 Once your video is uploaded, YouTube processes it. We now have to embed it into our website. Even before the processing is done, you'll see a message saying that the upload is complete. Below it, you'll see a box containing some code. Copy and paste this code into one of your web pages, where you want the video to appear.

4 Visitors to your website can now see the video when they look at your website, and can click the large play button overlaid on the video to play it.

Panoramic images

Panoramas give visitors the chance to see a place in its full glory and even conduct virtual tours. Here's how to turn those images around

A panorama can place a building in context within its landscape, or be used to show an entire room in one shot. You don't need special equipment – just a steady hand, a digital camera and a photo-editing package. Here we're using Adobe Photoshop CS2 to create a panorama automatically, but you can use any photo editor that supports layers to do it manually.

1 Take several shots of your subject. It's best to use a tripod, so all the shots line up perfectly, but you can do it freehand if you don't have one. Placing the camera on a static object such as a table can help. You can minimise the visibility of the join between images by locking the exposure settings and white balance on your camera; refer to your manual if you're not sure whether this is possible on your camera. This will help to eliminate contrast variations between photos.

2 Open Adobe Photoshop and select File, Automate, Photomerge. Select the files you want including and click OK, and Photoshop will attempt to stitch them

together. You may find that some photos cannot be processed and are left in the bar at the top of the page.

3 If Photoshop has managed to merge all your photos and the seams aren't overly visible, you can crop the image into a rectangle and then save it, ready for use. However, if some images haven't been added to the panorama, they can be dragged from the top toolbar and placed in position manually. Try to line up the images as closely as possible, and you'll find Photoshop snaps them into place. If a seam is noticeable, try dragging one image slightly and attempting the join again.

4 You can include the panorama as a normal image on your website. However, the MapLib tool gives visitors the chance to scroll around and zoom in or out of the image. Just register a free account at www.maplib.net and click on My Pictures to upload your image. You'll see the viewer, which is based on code from Google Maps. Click the Share tab to see the code, and cut and paste it where you want the image to appear on your website.

ESSENTIALS

SKILL LEVEL
Beginner
Intermediate
Expert

HOW LONG
1 hour 30 minutes

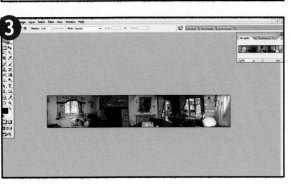

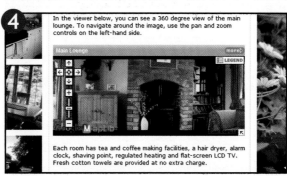

TIP
For the best-quality panoramas, use a tripod with the camera turned on its side. You'll end up with taller images that leave you more room to crop in on the final panorama.

MP3 players

If you're a musician, a website is a great way to draw attention to your work. It's easy to add a gadget enabling visitors to listen to your efforts

ESSENTIALS ●●●

SKILL LEVEL
Beginner
Intermediate
Expert

HOW LONG
20 minutes

For most budding musicians seeking to give their profiles a boost, a page at MySpace (www.myspace.com) will suffice. However, if you want something bespoke, a Google gadget such as the MP3 player we are using here will enable visitors to stream songs directly from your site.

Many sites play a MIDI file automatically when they load, but don't be tempted to do this on your site. The poor-quality files sound old-fashioned, and it's bad etiquette to play a song without first asking the visitor.

1 Upload an MP3 file to your web host using an FTP client, or via your site's Control Panel. This will be the file streamed every time a user clicks the Play button. For this reason, you should lower the quality of the file (by reducing its bit rate in an audio convertor) to speed up loading times and ensure you don't use up lots of bandwidth. Once the file is uploaded, you will need to make a note of its URL.

2 This free player provides a Play/Pause button and a progress bar, allowing a track to be played directly from your site. Go to http://tinyurl.com/mp3gadget. Click the 'Add to your webpage' button to get to the Preferences page.

3 Here you need to insert the URL for the file you wish to play on your site. Also, remove the text in the Title box; you're better off adding a title in your web page. Edit the height of the gadget to 55 pixels to remove the vertical scroll bar. Then change the colour of the border to match the colour scheme of your website.

4 Once you've finished editing the preferences of the gadget, click the Get the Code button and copy the code displayed in the text box. You'll need to paste this into your web page, where you want the MP3 player to appear. Once you've saved the HTML file, the media player should appear and work as you'd expect.

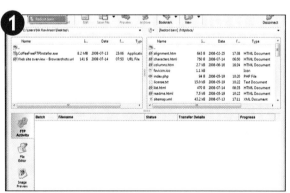

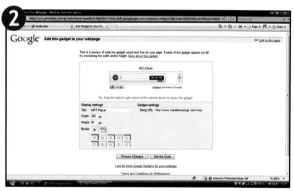

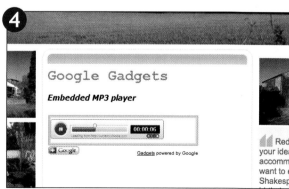

Driving directions

If visitors to your website need to know how to get somewhere, you can easily provide the tools necessary to show them the way

O ur Redcot Barn website is the perfect example of a website where driving directions are relevant. Rather than including a map of the local area as a JPEG image, you can easily add a driving directions gadget, thereby saving your visitors time and hassle.

1 Visit http://tinyurl.com/directionsgadget and click the 'Add to your webpage' button to load the configuration page.

2 First, change the default Location to the country in which you will be requiring directions. You should also change the Language in the drop-down box to your preferred language. In our example, the gadget will be used only to direct people to Redcot Barn, so the most important detail for us to include is the address, and this goes in the End Address box. A nice touch is to add a helpful message to the Start Address box so, for example, you could type 'Enter your postcode, eg DA4 2HW'.

3 The last step to customising the gadget is to change the colour and size of the box. If you're placing the gadget in a sidebar, you can tailor it to fit perfectly by editing its width and height. If the gadget is the focus of a page, you can leave the width at its default value, but it's worth increasing the height from 91 to 100 pixels to avoid the clutter of a vertical scrollbar.

Next choose a border for the box. You can add a title for the gadget, or leave the box empty if you don't need one. At any point, you can click the Preview Changes button to see how your options will look.

4 Once you've customised everything, click the Get the Code button to reveal the code in the text box below. Cut and paste this code into the page where you want the gadget to appear, and save the file. The resulting directions appear in a new browser window, since this gadget redirects visitors to Google Maps (see page 138 to find out how to add Google Maps to your website).

ESSENTIALS

SKILL LEVEL
Beginner
Intermediate
Expert

HOW LONG
30 minutes

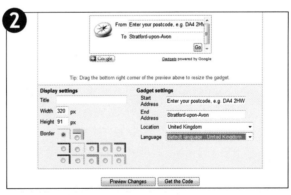

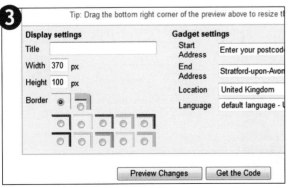

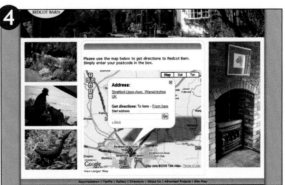

Weather forecasts

Including a weather forecast on your website is easy to do, won't cost a penny and is another helpful way to keep your visitors up to date

ESSENTIALS ●●●

SKILL LEVEL
Beginner
Intermediate
Expert

HOW LONG
30 minutes

Adding a weather forecast would be ideal for our Redcot Barn website, as potential customers can see at a glance what the local weather is like.

It's easy to add a forecast to your website using the myWeather gadget, which takes data from www.weather.com and displays it in an easy-to-read format. This is far better than updating your site every day by hand. Other weather widgets enable the user to change the location of the forecast, but the myWeather gadget allows you to fix the forecast area; this is useful if you want to prevent people searching for other forecasts.

1 Go to the myWeather gadget's homepage at http://tinyurl.com/myweather and click on the 'Add to your webpage' button to see the Preferences page.

2 To configure the gadget, you need to look up the location code of the area for which you want a weather forecast. Go to the myWeather website (www.notkewl.com/myWeather) and enter a UK town or city. The nearest town to Redcot Barn is Stratford-upon-Avon, which returns a code of UKXX1549. Copy and paste this code into the Zip/Location Code box on the gadget's configuration page. Click on the Preview Changes button to check the gadget is displaying the forecast for the next three days in Stratford-upon-Avon.

3 Delete the title, as you won't want this on your web page. Increase the height to 270 pixels to remove the vertical scroll bar. Most importantly for a UK-based forecast, select Metric Units in the drop-down box so temperatures are displayed in Celsius, not Fahrenheit.

4 Once you've customised everything and the gadget is showing the forecast for the correct area, click on the Get the Code button to display the code. Cut and paste this into your web page, where you want the forecast to appear.

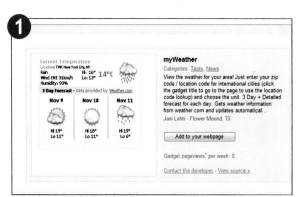

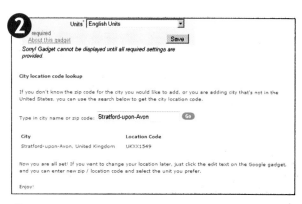

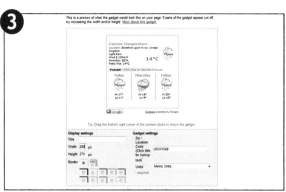

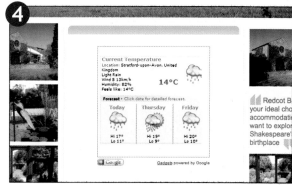

Photo slideshows

A slideshow is a charming way to showcase a selection of photos, and it doesn't take long to create a simple one using Picasa

Sometimes you'll want to show visitors to your site more than just a couple of photos, and that's when a slideshow works wonders. On page 128, we'll show you how to create a customised show using JavaScript, but here's how to create a simple slideshow using Picasa.

Picasa is a Google application for organising photos online. You can upload images, give them descriptions and arrange them into albums. You can also use Picasa to create slideshows for use on your website.

1 To create an online gallery, you'll need a Google account. Visit http://picasaweb.google.com/home and create a new account, or log in if you already have one. Accept the Terms and Conditions and click the Free Download button, if you haven't already installed Picasa.

2 In Picasa, create a new album by clicking on the Upload button. Add a title and any other details you want, and choose the Public or Unlisted option. On the next page, you'll be prompted to install the Picasa Uploader. Once this is installed, choose photos to upload. Next, click on to the album's page and make a note of the RSS feed address by right-clicking on the RSS link at the bottom of the page and choosing Copy Shortcut.

3 Go to http://tinyurl.com/picasagadget and click the 'Add to your webpage' button to see the Preferences page. Paste the feed you copied in Step 2 into the Picasa Web RSS Feed box on the Preferences page. Remove the text from the title box, and increase the size of the gadget so the image can be seen without cropping. View the effect of any changes made by clicking Preview Changes.

4 Once you're happy, click the Get the Code button and copy and paste the code into your web page, where you want the slideshow to appear. If you update the images in the Picasa Web Album, the new images will appear on your website automatically.

 ESSENTIALS

SKILL LEVEL
Beginner
Intermediate
Expert

HOW LONG
1 hour

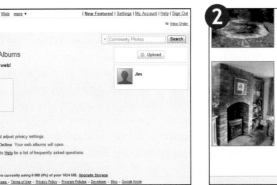

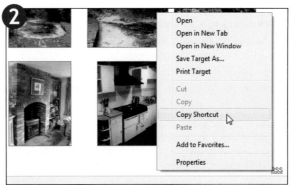

Make the most of RSS feeds

An RSS feed keeps people up to date with new content on your site, so that they know about fresh updates as soon as they happen

ESSENTIALS ●●●○

SKILL LEVEL
Beginner
Intermediate
Expert

HOW LONG
3 hours

RSS stands for Really Simple Syndication, or Rich Site Summary, depending on who you ask. Beyond the acronyms, an RSS feed is a way to view or publish frequently updated content such as news stories, blogs or podcasts.

Adding an RSS feed to your website lets your visitors keep up to date with news and events without having to check back continually to see if anything has been updated. Therefore, there's little point in including an RSS feed on a static website, where little of the content changes from day to day. RSS is better suited to news sites and blogs, where feeds can be used to alert readers each time a new story or blog post is uploaded. Similarly, RSS can be used to tell media player software such as iTunes when a new podcast is available.

The idea behind RSS is a complex one to get to grips with, but once you understand it, it soon becomes indispensable. An RSS feed is simply an XML file (XML being similar to HTML) that is stored on your web server. The file contains a list of the most recent articles, blog posts or podcast files on your site. When your visitors use an RSS feed application such as Google Reader on their PC, they can see at a glance if any of their favourite websites have been updated. It makes the task of keeping up with multiple websites a lot easier, and ensures that visitors never miss a new article.

CREATING A FEED

Adding an RSS feed to your website can be difficult, because it needs to be programmed to update automatically whenever you add a new post. Thankfully, you don't need to do this yourself. If you're using a blogging tool such as WordPress (see page 90) or a CMS such as Joomla (see page 94) for a news-based website, you'll almost certainly have an RSS feed already. If you don't, the easiest way to get one is to use a service that provides one (see the Tip opposite).

All you need to worry about, therefore, is changing the settings to suit your website. The most important aspect to consider is whether to include the full text of your posts in the feed. If you do, visitors won't need to go to your site to read the full details. Including just an excerpt will force them to go to your site to get the full story; this is a crucial manoeuvre if you intend to make money from advertising, or from the services or products that you provide. Having said that, adding the complete text to the feed makes it more convenient for readers.

There's only so much you can tweak from within your CMS, and the basic RSS feed has its limitations. If people aren't visiting your site to read the content, it can be hard to track the number of readers you have. There are free tools you can use to get more from your feed, though. In the walkthrough opposite, we'll take you through setting up and using the excellent FeedBurner. You'll need an RSS feed configured before you can do this.

Below: Google Reader is a good RSS feed application, and it is free to use

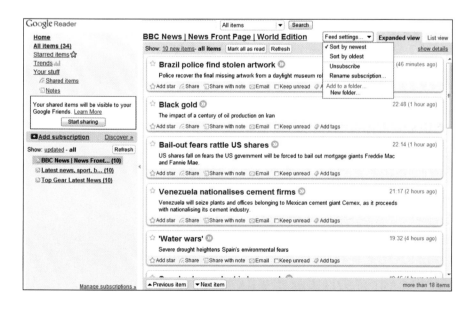

How to... Use FeedBurner to get more from your feed

1 Go to www.feedburner.com and enter the URL of your RSS feed. This can be found by right-clicking on the RSS link on your website and selecting Copy Link Location. Click Next and then enter a descriptive name for your feed. You will also need to choose a username and password on this screen in order to register a new account.

2 Once this is done, you will be given a new RSS feed address, which will be used instead of the standard feed on your site. This will allow you to use the advanced FeedBurner features, but will be completely transparent to your readers. Click on My Feeds at the top of the page once you have completed the registration process, then select the feed that you just created. You'll then be able to see how many people are reading your content, although it will take a day or so before you can see this figure.

3 Instead of using a plain-text link to this new RSS feed, FeedBurner can automatically create HTML that you can insert into your web pages to give you a more noticeable and attractive icon.

Click on the Publicize tab at the top of the page and then the 'Friendly graphic' link to reach the oddly named Chicklet Chooser. From here, you can select the style of icon you want to use, and simply cut and paste the code into the web page, where you want to include the RSS feed. Usually, this will be your homepage. Alternatively, you could choose to make it part of the header on your site, so it's visible on every page.

4 There are other ways that FeedBurner can publicise your new RSS feed and give your readers an easy way to stay up to date with your news and blog posts. Click on the Publicize tab again and select Email Subscriptions on the left. This will provide you with the code to place a small box on your site where users can sign up to receive email updates about your posts. This is perfect for those visitors who are unsure what RSS feeds are, or who don't want to install an RSS reader.

Checking back on FeedBurner periodically will allow you to track how many readers your RSS feed is attracting; this is something that a standard RSS feed alone doesn't provide. Be warned, though: checking statistics can become addictive.

TIP
To get an RSS feed for your site, you'll need additional services such as Blogger, WordPress or TypePad. To learn how to use their RSS features, visit http://tinyurl.com/aboutrss.

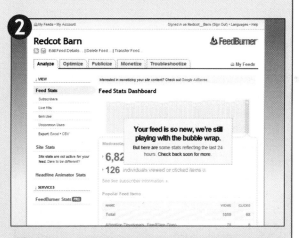

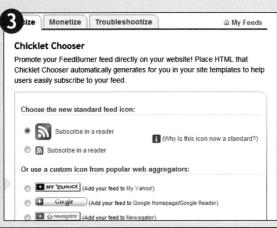

TIP
If you like the statistics FeedBurner provides, you'll probably like Google Analytics. See page 115 to find out how to use this useful tool.

Internet forums

Providing a place for a community to chat on your website is easy, and it won't cost a penny if you install some open-source software

Having a regular group of visitors to your site is great, but giving them a way to converse makes them stay on your site for longer, potentially earning you more advertising revenue, and it adds value for users who share a common interest. For example, if your website is for a local mums and toddlers' club, a forum offers a way for members to chat to each other, arrange meetings, swap tips and offer advice.

It's sensible practice to make people sign up with an email address and password, to prevent spam posts. To prevent libellous or nasty posts, you must also moderate the forum, or delegate the job to someone you trust.

In this walkthrough, we'll show you how to get a forum up and running using phpBB, a popular open-source forum program. You'll also need a web-hosting account with a MySQL database and PHP support.

1 See if your web host has an automatic installation service. Sometimes phpBB can be installed at the click of a button using a tool called Fantastico; look for it in your hosting provider's control panel. If you find it, use this install method and go to Step 7. If not, download the latest version of phpBB from www.phpbb.com/downloads and extract the files to a folder on your desktop.

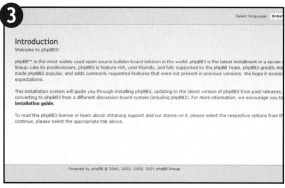

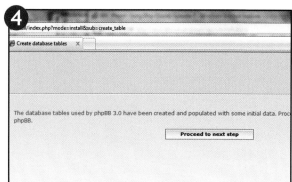

2 Next, upload the files to a new folder on your web server using your FTP software. If you don't have FTP access, upload the single zipped file using your host's file manager and then unzip the file from the online control panel.

3 Once the files are uploaded, you need to configure the installation. Open your browser and enter the address of your forum. This will be your domain name, followed by the name of the folder containing the phpBB files; in this instance, www.redcotbarn.co.uk/forum. This will take you to the main installation page for phpBB.

4 Click on the Install tab, then click on the 'Proceed to next step' button. This will take you to the requirements page for the installation, where phpBB will run several tests to see that you have all the appropriate features and permissions to run the software. Once these tests have been completed successfully, click the 'Start install' button at the bottom of the page.

5 On the Database settings page, you'll need to go back to your hosting account and create a database, which phpBB will use to store your users' details and their posts. If you're not sure how to create a database, contact your hosting provider. Name the database 'forum', without the quotes. Create a new user, assigning them read and write permissions on the database. Once you've done this, go back to the phpBB installation page and enter the database details. Proceed to the next page and enter the user details you just created.

6 The rest of the settings in the installation pages can be left at their default values. When all the steps are complete, you must delete the installation directory. If you don't do this, the forum won't be visible.

7 You'll then be taken to the Administration page. Here the forum can be customised and controlled when it's up and running. Only one thread is available by default. To add more, click on the Forums tab at the top of the page and then click the 'Create new forum' button before entering a name and description for the section.

The first time you create a forum, you need to assign permissions. These define who can do what on this part of the message board. It's best to assign the standard permissions to only registered users when you're starting out. You'll get a better idea of how to tailor this once your community starts to grow. With every thread you create from then on, you can select the permissions from an existing thread on the 'Create new forum' page by using the drop-down box.

8 You can now view your forum. Click on the 'Board index' link in the top right of the page. This will take you to the same page your visitors will see. You can place a link to this – either in the text of another web page or as a link in the main navigation bar – so visitors can access the forum without having to type its URL into the address bar in their browser. The forum will look plain at first but you can customise it, placing your own header on the page or using one of many phpBB themes that can be found online for free (see the Tip, below).

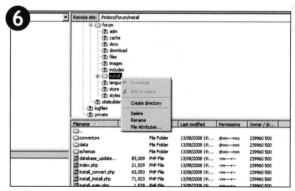

TIP
To spice up the look of your forum, browse the styles and themes at www.phpbb-styles.com, www.phpbb.com/styles and www.phpbb3styles.net.

Finishing touches

Now the bulk of your website's in order, there are just a few things left to consider to make it work for you. First, you must ensure there are no legal issues with the content you publish. Images, text, logos, audio and video can all be copyrighted, so you'll need to know the content is your own, or that you have permission to use it. We'll explain the pertinent details, so you stay on the right side of the law.

We'll also help you to improve the chances of visitors returning to your website. This is enormously beneficial, especially if you intend to sell products or services. We'll show you how to use your site to make money, even if it's just to cover hosting costs. Finally, we'll explain how you can check your site to ensure that it continues to look and work at its best.

Legal considerations

Before you publish anything online, be absolutely sure it won't land you in hot water with the law. We explain the main issues to bear in mind

Below: Flickr has plenty of Creative Commons material on its site, but bear in mind that not all of it is free to use

Even if your website is designed for the pleasure of your friends and family, you should never forget that the World Wide Web is exactly that. Unless you password-protect it, your site can be seen by anyone. For this reason, you need to be clued up on the law and fastidious about every single detail you publish online.

PROPERTY RIGHTS

First, you need to be familiar with the concept of copyright. Just because some text or an image is publicly accessible online, it doesn't mean anyone and everyone can copy and use it. Makers of commercial websites pay a lot of money for the words and photos that appear on them, and they won't take kindly to people ripping them off, even people who aren't out for commercial gain.

When you are looking for images to use on your site, it's best to assume that the pictures you find online are copyrighted unless you can prove otherwise: this is the best way to avoid expensive legal wrangling. However, there are ways to find legal-to-use images. Flickr (www.flickr.com) is a great place to find Creative Commons-licensed pictures (see the box below). Just remember that a copyright owner can waive their rights at their discretion. If you see an image that you simply must have, email the owner and politely ask permission. However, most professional photographers will charge you for using their images; it's their prerogative.

If you decide to go down the route of paying for the images on your site, you could try a microstock site. These are large image libraries that charge either per image or on a monthly or yearly basis for a set number of image downloads. Examples of image libraries are Shutterstock (www.shutterstock.com) and iStockPhoto (www.istockphoto.com). These sites allow you to buy photos for as little as 50p each. In return, you have the right to use the image on your site, although you can't then sell the image on to someone else.

The best way to avoid copyright issues altogether is to take your own pictures to use on your website. There are a few things to bear in mind, though. First, if you intend to make money from your images, make sure the people in them are happy about this. If a picture is primarily of one person, ask them first. If things are really taking off, it may be worth investigating a model release. This is a contract, signed by your subject, that allows you to sell the image. Remember that it's legal for you to take – and sell – pictures in public places, even if the resulting shots contain identifiable people.

ON YOUR MARKS

Trademarks are logos, symbols, images, words or phrases that are owned by a company. Even sounds can be trademarked; just think of the Intel Inside sound that accompanies TV adverts.

You should be careful of accidentally creating a website element that will remind people of a trademark. It will make you look unoriginal, and you certainly don't want to attract the attention of high-powered lawyers. You can even infringe a trademark with the URL that you choose for your site.

Some people register domain names that are almost identical to those of popular websites. For instance, www.whitehouse.org is the URL of a satirical website. This site gets plenty of hits simply because people haven't realised that they should have gone to www.whitehouse.gov, which is the real presidential address. However, if you try this tactic, it will be obvious that you're trying to pass yourself off as someone associated with the real site and the company may take legal action (see page 17 for details).

FREEDOM OF SPEECH

If you're running a news website, or anything that references current affairs, remember that quoting people is acceptable, as long as you cite your sources. Never make it appear as if an interviewee were talking directly to you if you're actually quoting words from another site.

Put simply, creating and running a website makes you a publisher, and so you should be mindful of the kinds of legal issues that can affect newspapers and magazines. The main one here is libel, which is where something written about someone is untrue and hurtful to that person's reputation. A good rule is to determine whether the story you're about to publish online is true. Have your checked your facts? Or are you publishing opinion without any facts behind it? Unless you have thousands of pounds to spare, you can't afford to get involved with any lawsuits.

Even repeating libellous claims is enough to get you into trouble. In 2007, Conservative MP Esther McVey

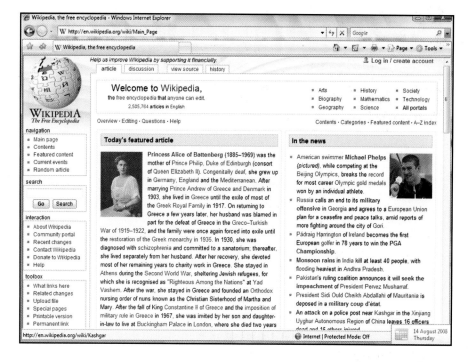

published claims about rival MP Stephen Hesford's plan to go on a taxpayer-funded sporting tour of Australia. He didn't intend to go. Although McVey was only repeating claims made in *The Mail on Sunday* months before, Hesford sued her.

AND FINALLY...

Remember that although running a website can give rise to legal confusion, most of it can be cleared up with a simple email. If in doubt, contact the person whose content you'd like to use; you may be surprised at how far this can get you. Beyond this, you can always consult a lawyer, although it will probably cost you. Of course, if you can't afford to consult a lawyer, you certainly can't afford to publish questionable material, so don't risk it.

Above: Wikipedia is a wealth of information that is free to all. You can do what you like with the content, as long as you credit your source, and make sure your final work has the same licensing restrictions as the original

Artistic licence Understanding Creative Commons

One way of avoiding the pitfalls of identifying content to use on your site is to find work licensed through Creative Commons. Creative Commons is an organisation that has developed a set of licence agreements that offer more flexibility.

Previously, work was either totally off-limits (copyrighted) or free-for-all (public domain), neither of which is particularly useful. Copyrighting work makes it too hard for people to use, and it reduces the chance of it finding a large audience. Conversely, however, public domain work is too easy to use, and reduces the chances of the author getting credited for the work they've done.

For more information, as well as a free set of icons to use if you decide to license your work with Creative Commons, you should visit www.creativecommons.org. Here are the main Creative Commons symbols to watch out for, and what they mean:

Content can be used, even for commercial gain. Derivative works can be made. Copyright must be attributed to author.

As above, but any work released must have the same Creative Commons licence as the original.

Content can be freely used, even for commercial gain. No derivative works. Original author must be cited.

As for attribution licence (top), with the added restriction that use must be non-commercial.

The most restrictive licence. No commercial use, no derivative versions and, of course, attribution.

Bringing people back to your website

A truly successful website relies on a steady, growing base of repeat visitors. Here's how to convince people to keep coming back

You've published your website and the visitors are pouring in, but to make sure your website is a hit you must secure repeat readers. While the number of unique hits (different visitors) is the figure advertisers look for in a website, you'll want people to keep coming back, whether you're selling goods or services, hoping to make your name as a blogger or creating an informative site that offers up-to-the-minute news and information.

If you run a small business, a professional-looking website can help mask the fact that your products are produced in your shed. That doesn't mean you should set out to mislead people, rather that you can gain their trust by providing valuable, accurate information. The way you conduct relationships with readers is important; it's better for your site to have a friendly atmosphere rather than a hard sell. After all, it's easier to sell to loyal customers than to acquire new ones.

KEEP IT TOPICAL

If you're a blogger, never forget that people search for newsworthy topics. During an election, for example, they'll search for the names of the candidates involved.

Right: Guardian.co.uk readers know that whenever they visit, the site will be up to date with the latest news and analysis

During big sporting events such as the Olympics or the World Cup, people search for the names of prominent performers, while the stars of new cinema releases are always a top search term on sites such as Google. If your readers get to know that they can count on you for the analysis of breaking stories, then they are more likely to make you their first stop whenever they come online.

The corollary of this is to keep your site updated. There's little more off-putting than realising the blog you're reading was last updated three months previously: the whole point of the format is that you keep people informed. If people find you don't update frequently, they simply won't bother coming back.

This brings us on to consistency of quality. People often start their websites with the greatest of care and the best intentions, only to find a year in that it has lost its allure. Lacklustre content is off-putting – people won't return to your site if they're uninspired by what they see.

JOIN THE CLUB

People will be more likely to return to your site if they have an incentive. A good way to create one, particularly if you have nothing to sell, is to create a community on your site. This is easy if you're making a site for a local club or church where people already know each other.

If you have a forum (see page 108) or host a blog (see page 90), you should get people to register before they post comments. This small action allows them to continue to voice their opinions on your site. Also, if you gather their email addresses, you'll be able to send out an email notifying them when your site's been updated. Just make sure you have a strong privacy policy, so people know how many emails they'll be receiving, and also that you won't give their addresses to anyone else. And remember, badgering people with spam certainly won't entice them to come back.

Understanding Google Analytics

Find out how many visitors your website is attracting and analyse their movements around your web pages with Google's invaluable tracker

Wouldn't it be great if you knew how many people were visiting your site every day? It would be even better to know which pages visitors were viewing, how long they spent reading each page and when they left your site. Using Google Analytics, you can find all this out free of charge. All you need is a Google account, which is also free. Analytics logs a small amount of information about the people that visit your site. It runs invisibly and, in most cases, has no effect on how fast your site loads or runs.

Go to www.google.com/analytics and sign in. If you don't already have an account through a service such as Google Docs or Gmail, you need to sign up first. Once you're logged in, Google will give you a small piece of JavaScript code to include on your site. Simply paste the code somewhere on your home page; the sidebar will do if you're using WordPress. Analytics takes a day to start reporting.

ANALYSE THIS

When you log in to Analytics, you'll see the Dashboard displayed prominently. The top graph shows the number of visitors per day. This is a useful number for telling, at a glance, whether traffic to your website is rising or falling, but there's a wealth of information besides this headline figure.

At the bottom right of the screen is the Content Overview, a useful panel that shows you which of the pages on your website are the most visited. This information can help you to figure out where you need to place advertising on your website for maximum effect. You can also give close attention to less frequently visited pages to try to determine what is wrong with them.

The navigation bar on the left is the best way to get around Google Analytics. For instance, click on Content, then Top Exit Pages. This view tells you which pages people looked at immediately before leaving your

website. If you spot a pattern, you can check the page or pages in question to see if there's anything obvious that might be causing people to leave. Perhaps you could add more links as a way to keep visitors interested for longer.

Traffic Sources is another helpful tool that can tell you which websites and search engines are directing traffic to your site. The search engine data is useful, as it tells you which keywords lead to your site, and how often they do so. This should help you optimise your website for search engines (see page 122 for more on this).

Finally, the Content tab has a small link called Site Overlay. This is one of Analytics' best tricks. It launches your website, with Analytics data pasted over the top, giving you a visual impression of where people are clicking when they're viewing your pages.

●●●● BENEFITS
- Determine the visiting patterns of the people coming to your website
- Find ways to improve your site so that people keep coming back

Below: Google Analytics is easy to use, phenomenally powerful and, best of all, it's free

Making money from your website

If you don't mind allowing some advertising on your site, you can turn your interest into a commercial venture and earn some cash

BENEFITS ●●●○○

- Pay your hosting fees using money from ads on your website
- Choose how many ads appear on your site, and customise them

If you're creating a website to promote a small business, money will be your ultimate goal. If you're making a website for a local club or about a particular hobby then profit probaby isn't high on your list of priorities, but that doesn't mean your website can't earn you a little pocket money. Hopefully, this will be enough to cover your hosting costs, plus something extra to reward you for the time and effort you've spent creating and maintaining it.

If you find that your website is receiving a large amount of traffic, you could turn this to your advantage, and approach companies whose products or services tie in with your site. However, it's unlikely that you'll be able to pull off any advertising deals like this unless your website receives many thousands of hits per month. Having said that, even if you have fewer visitors, you can still earn some revenue with the help of Google AdSense or an affiliate program such as Amazon Associates.

AdSense will pay a small amount every time a user clicks on targeted advertising on your site. You should bear in mind that small sites might earn only £50 per year – the minimum needed to withdraw cash from the scheme. The Amazon Associates scheme works in a similar way, by displaying adverts on your page, but it

shares with you a portion (up to 10 per cent) of any sales made as a result of people clicking on a particular advert.

Allowing adverts on your site is often a compromise. It's no secret that surfers don't like to be bombarded with advertising. Furthermore, adverts can clutter your pages and make them look untidy. But if you are careful and the adverts are subtle, they shouldn't put people off.

HOW TO... USE GOOGLE ADSENSE

1 Go to the homepage at www.google.com/adsense and create an account; a normal Google account won't do. You'll need to provide details such as your name and address. You can then set up a banner ad for your site. Click on the AdSense Setup tab at the top of the main page. Here you'll see various ways to earn revenue from AdSense. We'll be using the AdSense for Content option, which produces banner advertising for products and services related to the content of your site.

2 On the AdSense for Content page, you're given two options: Ad units and Link units. Ad units are used to give actual adverts, either text-only or image-based, while Link units are used to give text links to broader topics that take the user to a page of search

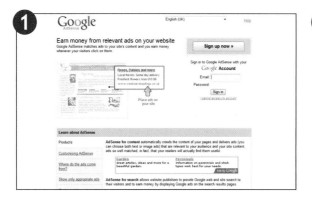

How to... Use Amazon Associates scheme

The Associates scheme lets you earn up to 10 per cent of any sales made when a visitor clicks on an Amazon advert on your site and subsequently makes a purchase. You can choose which products to promote from the millions in Amazon's catalogue.

1 First you need to register an account with the Amazon Associates scheme by visiting the homepage at http://tinyurl.com/amazonassociates.

2 Once you have created an account, go to the Associates Central page and click the Build Links/Widgets link on the left-hand side of the site to see the different types of adverts that you can create. Some options are as simple as text links to products on the Amazon website, and these are particularly useful for targeted items. So for our holiday cottage website, we might choose to display a link to a popular tourist guidebook of the local area.

Other options are more complex, such as the Self-Optimising Links option that we're using here. This works in the same way as the customisation options in AdSense, by tailoring the banner to suit the content of the site on which it appears.

3 Click on the 'Add to your Web page' button below the Self-Optimising Links option, and you will see the configuration page for the widget. On this page, you can adjust the dimensions and colour of the banner. You'll see a warning if you change it too much, as Amazon requires the advert to be recognisable. You can also choose whether to show the Amazon logo, product images or a border.

4 Once the banner is ready, copy and paste the code from the box below the configuration tool into your site. The optimisation means that the adverts will become more relevant over time.

results. On the Redcot Barn site, an Ad unit will provide links to specific guest houses and a Link unit will redirect to search pages for guest houses. We're selecting Ad units.

3 The next page offers several customisation options. These allow you to change the appearance of the ad box to fit in with the colour scheme and layout of your site. We're making the border of our banner green to blend in with the Redcot Barn website. An advert that looks out of context is unlikely to get many clicks. Once you're ready, click the Submit and Get Code button.

4 Cut and paste the code into your site, where you want the ad box to appear. Google will analyse the content of that page and put relevant adverts in the box. Log in to the AdSense page periodically to see how much your advert is earning, and make any changes. AdSense lets you tweak banners without having to re-insert code.

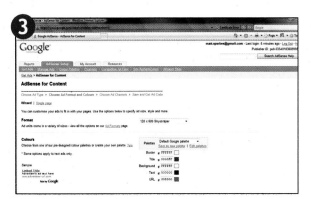
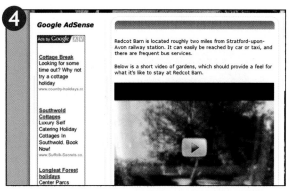

Maintaining your website

Even if you don't intend to update your website every day, a little maintenance from time to time will ensure it keeps running smoothly

It's important to conduct regular MOTs of your website to make sure everything is working correctly. It may be that there are problems with your images or code, and other issues can occur over time. A website that you link to may disappear, leaving a broken link, or a new browser version may be released that doesn't work with certain page elements. A tune-up tool can help you check the health of your site. In this walkthrough, we're using NetMechanic HTML Toolbox.

1 The free trial for NetMechanic is limited to testing just five pages of your website. However, this should give you a pretty good idea of how the tool works, and you can then decide if you want to buy it. Visit www.netmechanic.com and click on the More link below the Evaluate column. Once the page loads, select Try it on the right-hand side.

2 On this page, you need to enter the address of the website that you want to test. You also need to enter an email address so you can receive the results of the test. Click the Test Now button once you've filled in these details. You'll then be taken to a confirmation page. You can close this, as the results of your test will be emailed to you within a few minutes.

3 Once you receive the email confirmation, you can follow the link that it contains to see the full results of your test. You can see that our site has several errors; these are intentional, to highlight how well the tool works. While there are no bad links, there are problems with the HTML, browser compatibility issues and pages taking too long to load because the images are too large. From this page, you can click on the Detailed Report link next to any error to see more details on the problem.

4 First, we'll look at the HTML Check & Repair results. Fortunately, there are no problems with our code. If problems are flagged up, they may not manifest themselves on all browsers; pages could appear fine to a visitor who uses Safari, but display incorrectly in Internet Explorer. In the free trial of NetMechanic, any problems are highlighted as pink for warnings and red for errors. In the full version, the problems are corrected automatically for you.

5 If you go back to the main results page, you can look at the browser compatibility results. Our site has some minor compatibility problems. Each element of the page that isn't compatible with all major browsers is listed here, along with a figure for the percentage of

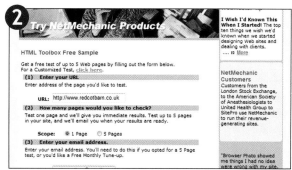

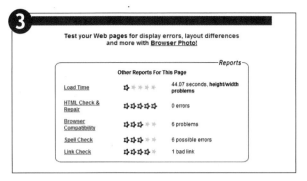

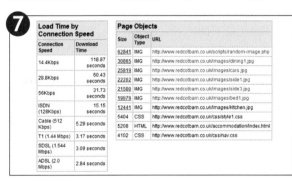

users who will be affected because their browser doesn't support that particular element. The test suggests that if this figure rises above 10 per cent, it becomes a serious problem, and that element should be replaced.

A browser calculator is also included here, so you can enter the exact breakdown of your visitors and the browsers that they use. Stick with the figures provided, unless you care only about visitors using Internet Explorer, for example. This way, you can improve your ratings by ignoring problems with other browsers.

6 Go back to the main results page to view the results of the spellcheck. Small spelling errors on your website can be a serious problem, as we explained on page 39; they convey the impression that the site has been badly prepared or put together with a lack of care, and the effect is amateurish. This automated spellcheck will highlight any words that it doesn't recognise and offer alternatives. However, it's not always spelling mistakes that are picked up; brand names and technical terms can confuse the spellcheck. Here, the word 'blog' isn't recognised and 'bog, log and bloc' are suggested.

While you may not always use the spellcheck's suggestions, it's useful for catching genuine errors.

7 Another important test is the load-time trial. It's important to strike the right balance between having a well-featured site with lots of images and pages that load quickly. Here, you can see that our site loads quickly (in less than three seconds) on a fast ADSL broadband connection, but on an ISDN line it takes over 15 seconds. This is because of the large images used – highlighted in the results. The tool recommends that the page is split into several smaller pages, or that the images are reduced in size.

8 The results provide lots of other useful pointers about your site, helping you to keep things running smoothly. If you have five pages or fewer, the free trial of NetMechanic will test your whole site for free. However, buying the full version gives even more options. It can be set to test your site periodically – once a week, for example – and email you the results. If you update your site regularly, this can be very reassuring.

Advanced projects

Using the information acquired so far, you're well on your way to creating an attractive, well-designed website with gadgets such as those mentioned in Chapter 7. However, to make your site even better, there are more advanced techniques you can use.

Most projects in this chapter involve programming in PHP and JavaScript. It's well worth the effort, as you'll find out how to add customised, interactive features such as Google Maps and create boxes with rounded corners. We'll also show you how to make random images appear on pages, resize image sizes automatically and create a full-screen slideshow with transitions. Also, to ensure you get as many hits as possible, we'll show you how to optimise your site to improve its ranking in search engines such as Google.

Improving your search ranking

Make sure your site has prime position in the results pages of search engines such as Google and you're sure to get more visitors

ESSENTIALS ●●●

SKILL LEVEL
Beginner
Intermediate
Expert

HOW LONG
2-4 hours

If you want as many people as possible to find your website, you need to do a few extra jobs to ensure your site ranks highly on search results. It's easy to add your site to search engines so friends or people with similar interests can find it. You must have a publicly visible website, such as www.redcotbarn.co.uk, to be able to add it to a search engine, so dedicated web hosting is essential (see page 12 for details). If your site is hosted for free and you don't have your own unique domain, you won't be able to do this project.

Web search engines are capable of searching through content from all over the internet almost instantly. Google knows what's on all these web pages, and can search through them so quickly because it holds a huge index of the words and phrases found on all the pages. This index works in much the same way as the index in a book, which lists words alphabetically, so you can quickly find the word you're looking for and, hence, the pages in which the word appears. Search engines all work differently, but there are three main steps used by them all: crawling, indexing and searching.

DISCOVERY CHANNELS

Crawling is the process by which search engines find out about new and updated web pages that need to be added to the index. Billions of pages from all over the internet have to be visited and downloaded. This is usually achieved by an automated computer program that runs on a large number of computers. These programs are called spiders or bots. The crawling process begins with a list of URLs generated from previous crawl processes and new websites submitted by webmasters. As the spider visits each of the web pages in the list, it records the links found and adds them to the list of pages to be visited.

The web pages are downloaded, analysed and broken down into words and phrases, which are stored in the

index. The index also takes note of special content in the web page, such as the title. This content can improve the search accuracy and present excerpts in the search results. The indexing process can extract information from sources other than HTML web pages, such as images and even Flash files.

KEY CONCERNS

Searching involves matching the keywords that are searched for against words and phrases from the index to find relevant web pages. Each search engine has a different method for calculating which are the most relevant results. The factors for what makes one result more relevant than another can be quite complicated and are often a well-kept secret. Since Google is the most popular search engine, we'll concentrate here on how to improve your rankings with Google.

Adding your own website to a search engine for crawling is simply a matter of going to the submission page, such as www.google.com/addurl for Google,

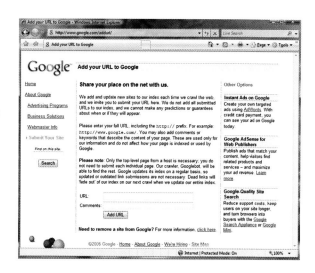

Right: It's quite easy to add your site to Google's web-crawling system

http://search.yahoo.com/info/submit.html for Yahoo! and http://search.msn.com/docs/submit.aspx for Microsoft's Live Search. There's no charge for this, but you'll have to wait a few days for the crawler to visit your website and update the indexes before your site appears in the search results.

Each search engine uses a different set of rules to decide which web pages are most relevant to a search query, so it's difficult to work out how to make your own website rank well. However, you can strategically design or modify web pages so they achieve a good ranking in search results. This is known as search engine optimisation (SEO). As many companies rely on their website appearing highly in search results, SEO has become a lucrative business.

Search engine providers generally disapprove of people trying to beat the system and artificially improve their search ranking. Still, by following some simple guidelines it's easy to ensure that your website can be successfully crawled and indexed.

● Use a descriptive <title> tag in each of your web pages. Search engines will use this tag as a source of important information about your page, and will often use it as the basis for the link in their results pages.

● Add a meta description to your web pages. This should describe the page in greater detail than the title, and may be used by the search engine to generate the excerpt in the results page. The meta description tag should be added to the <head> tag in the HTML page, so for example:

```
<html>
  <head>
    <title>Redcot Barn Holiday Home
    </title>
```

```
<meta name="description" content="
 This is the home page for Redcot
 Barn. View accommodation, facilities,
 location and prices.">
 </head>
</html>
```

● Use <h1> and <h2> tags as well as bold fonts to pick out headings and emphasise text. Search engines will identify these tags as a source of significant keywords and will increase the relevancy score when searches are made using them. Don't repeat keywords in hidden parts of the page that the user cannot see in a bid to fool the indexer. Search engines can detect this; their reputation is based on the quality of their results. In the worst-case scenario, the search engine will discover what you are up to and remove your website from the index completely.

CALLING OFF THE SEARCH

Sometimes you'll need to prevent search engines crawling and indexing content from certain parts of your website. You might want to do this if certain web pages contain information that you don't want to make searchable, or if you have web pages that link to many gigabytes of data. Search engine crawlers tend to use a lot of bandwidth as they download all the reachable content on your website, so it's easy to exceed the maximum bandwidth limit of a hosted website by having lots of content available. Exceeding your bandwidth limit can make your website become temporarily unavailable or lead to expensive hosting bills.

In these cases, add a special file to the root of your website, called robots.txt. This gives instructions to the search engine crawlers about which parts of your website should not be processed. A simple robots.txt file that

Top left: Adding a meta description tag, which describes the content of a web page, helps to ensure that Google shows your site when people search for the same terms

Top right: Use HTML heading tags to emphasise keywords since search engines will pick up on these

Left: Google Webmaster
Tools will help you select
which pages on your site
are searchable

Right: Webmaster Tools
will also help you diagnose
problems with your site, and
provide tips on how to improve
your ranking

Left: Google Webmaster Tools will help you select which pages on your site are searchable

Right: Webmaster Tools will also help you diagnose problems with your site, and provide tips on how to improve your ranking

prevents crawlers processing specific files and directories looks like this:

```
User-agent: *
Disallow: /tmp/
Disallow: /images/
Disallow: /old/index.html
```

The first line allows you to give instructions to a particular crawler. Using * indicates that the rules should be applicable to all crawlers. The following lines are rules that prevent the crawling of specific directories and files. It's easy to drastically alter the content indexed by a search engine by changing this file, sometimes by more than you intended, so be careful with your changes.

MASTER PLAN

Google has a set of free tools called Webmaster Tools, which can help you create a robots.txt file and get more information about which parts of your website are being indexed. Webmaster Tools allow you to find out more about how Google (and hence other search engines) sees your website. They also help diagnose problems that are preventing pages being searchable, and improve your overall search visibility. You just need an active Google account, which is easy to create. Once you have an account, log on to the Webmaster Tools homepage at www.google.com/webmasters/tools. After you've logged in, you can add URLs for the websites that you want to use the tools on, such as www.redcotbarn.co.uk.

You can type in any URL, even those you do not own or control, which is a security problem. Before you can use the tools on a particular website, you have to prove to the tools that you are in charge of it (see box, left).

Once your website is verified, you can access the full set of tools. These are divided into five main sections: diagnostics, statistics, links, sitemaps and tools. The first section, diagnostics, is where you can find out about any errors that Google encountered when crawling your website, such as broken links or pages with missing titles.

You can also see an overview of pages that were excluded by the robots.txt file to ensure that you have it set up correctly. Ideally, you'll want as few errors as possible, so you should check this report often.

The statistics section provides various reports, including what kinds of searches people are using to find your website and an overview of keywords found in your indexed web pages. You can also see a list of the top phrases used in external links to your site, such as in anchor tags. Google is interested in how other people link to your site and includes this information in its relevancy calculations. The Links section provides much more information about external links to your website.

Sitemaps are meta data files you can add to your website to describe its layout, ensuring that crawlers can find pages they might otherwise miss. This is particularly useful if you have web pages with dynamic content, using JavaScript to create page links, or pages that don't have links to them. The sitemaps section in the Webmaster Tools allows you to upload and manage sitemaps. For more information and a wizard to get you started, see www.xml-sitemaps.com.

The final section, tools, has several useful utilities, including a page to create and analyse robots.txt files. Here you can make sure your robots.txt file is up to date and test any changes before uploading a new file. You can use the 'Remove URLs page' option to resolve issues with pages that no longer exist, or those that create problems by being in the Google index.

ONWARDS AND UPWARDS

Although SEO is a complicated subject, you're now armed with the knowledge of how search engines work, so you should be able to lift your site up their rankings. Using utilities such as Google Webmaster Tools, you can create a custom robots.txt file to fine-tune the way the crawling process interacts with your website. You'll find plenty of information online with more tips for targeting specific search engines. Just remember: keep it simple, and let the search engines do the hard work for you.

TIP

To prove you own your website, upload an empty file to it or paste a meta tag into the <head> section of your home page. The information you need will be supplied by Google and looks like:

```
<meta name="verify-
v1" content="2Q7fj
HeYmi=">
```

When you've added it, ask Google to match the details it supplied against the meta tag on your site's home page. This will prove you are the owner of the site.

Displaying random photos on your site

You can display photos to make your site look fresh for returning visitors, even if nothing else has changed since they last looked at it

●●●● (ESSENTIALS

SKILL LEVEL
Beginner
Intermediate
Expert

HOW LONG
2 hours

An important step in making your website look professional is to make it dynamic, which means certain elements are created only when the visitor clicks a link to the page. This is usually achieved using a scripting language and a database. PHP is a popular scripting language that can extract content from a database. It runs on a web server, generating standard HTML pages that are sent to the visitor's web browser, allowing any browser to view a page with PHP scripts. PHP files are normal text files, so you can do all your PHP work using Windows' built-in Notepad. However, these files must end in .php.

Here we'll show you how to write a simple script to show a random photo. You'll need to download the files from our website (see Tip, right) to do this project.

GETTING STARTED

Create a folder called 'scripts' in the server's root and upload the common.php file. Create a folder called randomimage and upload the remaining files and images folder here. Open Notepad and test-page.php, and you'll see a file that looks like normal HTML, except there's a block of code in the middle:

```php
<?php
   require "../scripts/common.php";
   $randomImage = getRandomImagePath
   ("./images");
?>
<p><?php
   echo "<img src=\"$randomImage\">";
?></p>
```

The `<?php` starts a new block of PHP code; the `?>` ends it. As you can see, there are two blocks of PHP code. The first block uses 'require' to include another PHP file

stored in the scripts folder in the server's root folder. It's this file that contains the function (that is, reusable code that does a specific job) for showing the random image. You should save your PHP functions into separate files, so you can reuse them in other scripts later.

The second line of the script does the work. It uses the `getRandomImageInPath()` function to search the folder we're using (`"./images"`) for a picture. It stores the file's name in the `$randomImage` variable. A variable is a virtual storage box for data, and anything starting with a $ is a variable. The second block of code uses the 'echo' command to output an HTML img tag using the contents of our variable as the image source.

INSIDE THE COMMON.PHP FILE

If you open the common.php file, you'll see that it contains many functions. These are all used to display a random function. The first is the getRandomImagePath that we used in the test-page.php file:

```php
function getRandomImagePath($aDirectory)
{
   $imagePaths = getImagesInPath
   ($aDirectory);
   $size = count($imagePaths);
   if($size > 0)
   {
      $randomIndex = mt_rand(0, $size
      - 1);
      return $imagePaths[$randomIndex];
   }
   else
   {
      return false;
   }
}
```

TIP
The examples we have used should work regardless of your web-hosting package. To save you having to type in our examples, all the files are available for download from www.redcotbarn.co.uk/advancedprojects/randomimage.
Here you will also find the working demonstrations. To try the test files on your web server, you'll need to use the same directory structure as we have.

The image shows a Windows Internet Explorer window titled "Random image in HTML" displaying a photograph of a house and garden viewed through a wooden structure.

Above: a random image can help to keep your website looking fresh for anyone who visits on a regular basis

This function stores the folder it is passed in the $aDirectory variable. The next line calls a function named getImagesInPath with our folder to create an array of all the images found. This is stored in the $imagePaths variable. Arrays are indexed lists, where each entry can be accessed through its index number; $imagePaths[0] refers to the first item in the list, as arrays are indexed from 0, not 1.

NUMBER CRUNCHING

Next, the built-in count() function is used to see how big the list is and store its size in the $size variable. It then checks to see if $size is greater than 0. If it isn't, the list is empty and false is returned. If it is greater than 0, the script needs to pick a random image from the list. A random number is stored in the $randomIndex variable. This uses the built-in mt_rand() function, which creates a random image between its two inputs; 0 is the first entry and $size -1 is the last. The image stored at $randomIndex using $imagePaths[$randomIndex] is returned to the calling script. To create the list of images, the getImagesInPath function looks like this:

```
function getImagesInPath
  ($aDirectory)
{
    if ($handle = opendir($aDirectory))
    {
```

```
    while (($filename = readdir
      ($handle)) !== false)
    {
        $nextPath = "$aDirectory/
          $filename";

        if(isJpegFile($nextPath))
        {
            $imagePaths[] = $nextPath;
        }
    }

    closedir($handle);
    }
    return $imagePaths;
}
```

This function attempts to open the folder in the $aDirectory variable using the built-in opendir() function. If this folder can't be accessed, false is returned. Otherwise, the script returns a handle, needed to access the files. It's stored in the $handle variable. Next, there's a while loop, which operates like this: while a statement is true, every instruction inside the loop is performed. This is used to read through the folder and examine each file. The function readdir($handle) reads a file and stores the result in a variable called $filename. It returns false when all files have been read, and this is the cue to cancel the loop.

NEXT IN LINE

For each file that is read, the $nextPath variable is used to store the folder and filename. The script checks to see if the file stored in $nextPath is a JPEG using the isJpegFile() function. If it is, the result is stored in an array called $imagePaths; the empty square brackets mean 'create a new list entry'. Then, closedir($handle) closes access to a file. When the while loop has ended, the list of JPEG files is returned. IsJpegFile uses two functions:

```
function isJpegFile($aPath)
{
    if(is_file($aPath))
    {
        return endsWith(strtolower
          ($aPath), ".jpg");
    }
    else
    {
        return false;
    }
}

function endsWith($aString, $aSuffix)
{
```

TIP

If you need a more detailed explanation of the PHP commands that are used here, you will find excellent documentation online if you visit www.php.net/docs.php.

```
$stringLength = strlen($aString);
$suffixLength = strlen($aSuffix);
if($stringLength < $suffixLength)
{
   return false;
}

$endOfString = substr($aString,
 $stringLength - $suffixLength);
return $endOfString == $aSuffix;
   }
?>
```

The first function takes a path to a file. It checks if there is a file using `is_file()`. If there is, it finds out if it ends with .jpg using the `endWith()` function. Everything is converted to lower-case using `strtolower()`, to avoid complications from upper-case characters. This is important if you use a Linux-based web host; file and folder names are case-sensitive in Linux, but not Windows.

The `endsWith` function works out the length of the string and the length of the suffix that is being searched for. The file's suffix is separated and stored in the `$endOfString` variable. This is done using `substr` (sub-string), which takes two arguments: the string that needs breaking up, and the numerical character position of the start of the break. This returns just the suffix. Next, `$endOfString == $aSuffix` is returned. This returns true if they match and false if they don't.

It's now easy to write a function to look for other file types. If you wanted `isGifFile()` you would create it in the same way, but you would use the line `return`

`endsWith(strtolower($aPath, ".gif")`. A neater solution is to have a PHP script that can be integrated into an HTML page. Visit www.redcotbarn. co.uk/advancedprojects/randomimage to see it in action. The code for the page uses `{img src="random-image.php"}`. Random-image.php acts as an image file. If you view its code in Notepad, you'll see it uses the same code and `getRandomImagePath()` function as the first example.

The remaining code makes the PHP file act like an image file. `$handle = fopen($imagepath, 'rb')` opens the physical JPEG file. The 'header' code is used to tell a web browser there's a JPEG coming, where it's stored and how big it is. As a different image is required each time, this code also tells the browser not to store the file in its cache. The `fpassthrough()` line tells PHP to stream the contents of the file to the browser – in other words, to send the JPEG image through.

GOING FURTHER

You now have code that you can use more than once in multiple web pages. You will probably want to modify this project to suit the way your website works. If you're using different folders to us, just update the path to the common.php file. You'll also need to point people towards the directory where you keep your images.

This project can be extended to look for different image types such as GIFs. You could also make your script look for both JPEGs and GIFs. You could use an OR statement to see if a field is a JPEG file or GIF file. If you get stuck, you may well find the help you need by reading the PHP documentation.

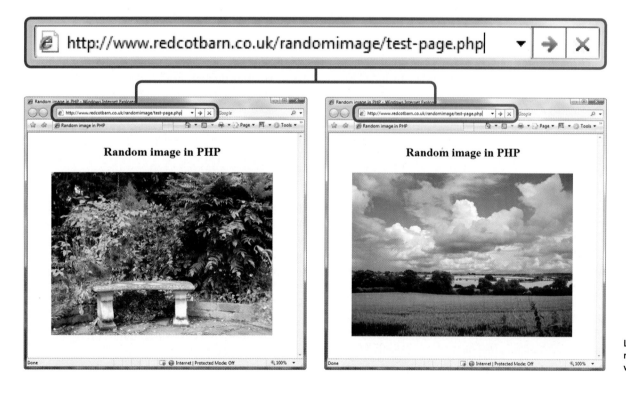

http://www.redcotbarn.co.uk/randomimage/test-page.php

Left: Each time the page is refreshed, a random image will be displayed

Making a slideshow for your website

The right slideshow can bring a touch of class to your website. Here we show you how to create a sophisticated online slideshow using PHP

ESSENTIALS ●●●

SKILL LEVEL
Beginner
Intermediate
Expert

HOW LONG
2 hours

TIP
Dedicated web hosting isn't required for this project, but it's recommended so that you can use PHP scripts to automate the slideshow setup. We used Fasthosts Home account (www.fasthosts.co.uk), which costs £3.99 per month.

On page 125 of this chapter, we showed you how to write a PHP script to display random photos on your website. However, sometimes you'll want to show more than just one photo. A slideshow is an efficient and effective way for visitors to see a selection of images. On page 105, we showed you how to create a simple slideshow with Picasa. In this project, we're going to go further and create a customised slideshow using JavaScript.

Using JavaScript, you can create stunning slideshows that work in any web browser without requiring plug-ins or extensions. A few years ago, web-based slideshows were static and dull, or written in Flash. While there's nothing wrong with Flash, it can sometimes limit the accessibility of your website, as users need a browser that supports it and must download a plug-in for it to work. These days, web browsers have excellent CSS support, while the maturity of modern JavaScript libraries means you can create appealing slideshows directly in HTML.

CHOOSING A JAVASCRIPT LIBRARY

There are many JavaScript libraries dedicated to creating slideshows. One of the best is TripTracker, which can be found at http://slideshow.triptracker.net. TripTracker is free to use as long as the script is not used for profit, so it's perfect for personal home pages. JavaScript is normally stored in separate files and not in the HTML, but the scripts for setting up these slideshows are so simple it is easier to include them directly in a page of HTML using a script tag. It's only worth saving the script as a separate file if you need to reuse the same slideshow on a different page.

The TripTracker library allows you to create a slideshow that displays a series of photos, using pictures stored on your website. Once launched, the slideshow presents each photo using the full size of the web browser window, scaling down the images if necessary.

The slideshow adjusts itself to suit the sizes of the images you use and the size of the monitor on which images are viewed. Bear in mind that this image scaling takes place in the web browser itself. Don't upload photos directly to your website from your digital camera without resizing them first, or else everyone who looks at your website will have to wait while huge photos are downloaded.

To add a slideshow to an HTML page, you first need to add a reference to the TripTracker JavaScript library. Usually, it's a good idea to download the JavaScript library and add it to your own website. However, in this case we recommend adding a reference in your HTML that points to the TripTracker website. This way, you will ensure that you're always using the latest version of the slideshow library; it's periodically updated with new features and bug fixes, such as adding support for the latest web browsers such as Internet Explorer 8.

Add the slideshow library with the following script tag (as we've done in simple.html at www.redcotbarn.co.uk/advancedprojects/slideshows/simple.html):

```
<script type="text/javascript" src="
http://slideshow.triptracker.net/
slide.js"></script>
```

Next, you need to set up the slideshow with the images you want shown. This is done as another script block, usually using images that are stored on your site, although you can use images from another site if you prefer. In simple.html you'll see a slideshow that shows a series of JPEG images. The script tag looks like this:

```
<script type="text/javascript">
  var slideshow = new PhotoViewer();
  slideshow.add('images/garden/
   flowers1.jpg');
  slideshow.add('images/garden/
```

24/30

Local intranet | Protected Mode: Off   🔍 100% ▾

```
    flowers2.jpg');
</script>
```

The first line of code (after the `<script>` tag) creates a PhotoViewer object that represents the slideshow and its configuration. Once you have the slideshow object, just add paths to the images you want to show. In our example, the images are stored in a directory called images/garden. It's a good idea to keep all your images in folders with descriptive names, so you'll know where to find things. Once you've added all the photos, you're almost done.

STARTING THE SLIDESHOW

You now need a way to start the slideshow. Usually, you would do this by making visitors click on an HTML link, but you can easily do it by making the slideshow a link from an image or another HTML element. The HTML for starting the slideshow from a link looks like this:

```
<a href="javascript:void(slideshow.
show(0))">View the slideshow</a>
```

This calls the `show()` function on the slideshow object we created earlier. The 0 in brackets is the parameter that is passed to the show method, and determines where you want the slideshow to start. Usually this will be 0, since you want to start with the first image. The examples at www.redcotbarn.co.uk/advancedprojects/slideshows will show you what the slideshow looks like.

You're not limited to one slideshow per page, either; you can add as many as you like. The trick is to create multiple PhotoViewer objects with different names. In our example, we've called the PhotoViewer object 'slideshow' as defined by the line that starts `var slideshow`. We've put an example of multiple slideshows on a page on our website. Here, you'll see two slideshows in the same HTML page. The benefit of having multiple slideshows on one page is that you

Above: The TripTracker slideshow in action on our website

> **TIP**
> Follow our examples by visiting www.redcotbarn.co.uk/advancedprojects/slideshows.

can group photos into albums, without the need to create a separate web page for each slideshow.

CUSTOMISING THE SLIDESHOW

There are several ways to customise your slideshows. One tool lets you add a caption and date to each photo. This appears underneath the image by the navigation controls. Click the 'Slideshow with captions' link on our website for an example.

The only additions to the code are extra parameters for the `add()` function on PhotoViewer. The caption and date are both optional parameters, so you can add both, or just a caption. The following line does both:

```
slideshow.add('images/garden/flowers
1.jpg', 'Small Yellow Flowers',
'12/10/2008 15:35');
```

Below left and right: One of TripTracker's benefits is full-screen photos

Customising the animation of the slideshow is also easy. Just use extra functions after you've defined all the pictures you want to use. These functions are called in the same way as the `add()` function, and are in the style '<nameofyourslideshow>.<nameoffunction>'.

The most useful setting is `setSlideDuration`, which, as it implies, is used to control how long each slide is shown in milliseconds. The default is 4000, which means each photo remains onscreen for four seconds.

The animated effect used as a transition from one slide to the next can be turned off. The slideshow uses a panning and fading effect, which can be turned off by calling `disablePanning()` and `disableFading()`. Other options are `enableAutoPlay()`, which causes the animation to start when the user clicks the link to the slideshow, and `enableLoop()`, which makes the slideshow loop indefinitely. Look at 'Slideshow with custom animation' on our website see a slideshow playing automatically without any panning and fading effects.

You can also change the background and shade effect colour, by calling `setBackgroundColor(colour)` and `setShadeColor(colour)`. Colours are defined using standard web hexadecimal numbers, with the default value #000000 (black). Go to

http://en.wikipedia.org/wiki/Web_colors for a list of hexadecimal web colours. If you don't like the shade effect, remove it by calling `disableShade()`. The default for the image caption is 10 pixels. Change this to 12 or 14 by calling `setFontSize(size)`. Click on 'Slideshow with custom appearance' on our website for an example that uses a different shade of background colour and a larger font.

You can change the toolbar that controls the playback. The 'photo link' and 'email photo link' buttons allow users to view the photo directly or email a link of the photo to a friend with their email client. You can remove these buttons by calling the `disableEmailLink()` and `disablePhotoLink()` functions. Remove the whole toolbar by calling `disableToolbar()`. You can even configure what the slideshow does when you click on it with the mouse. The default is to close the slideshow. Using `setOnClickEvent(slideshow.startSlideShow)` causes the slideshow to play when you click on it, and `setOnClickEvent(slideshow.permalink)` shows the current photo in a new window. Click on 'Slideshow with custom controls' on our website for an example that removes the toolbar and sets the slideshow to start playing when you click on it.

IMPLEMENTING PHP

Part of the PHP script used on page 125 is able to find all the images in a directory, which you can reuse here to set up a slideshow more quickly. You can use that script, common.php, which is available in the 'Display random images' section of Advanced Projects on our website. The benefit of using PHP to make slideshows is that you can upload new images to your website and have them appear automatically in your slideshow, without having to update the HTML manually.

Create a PHP file with the .php extension containing the following script (see automatic.php, which is included in the sample files for slideshows on our website):

```
<script type="text/javascript">
    var slideshow = new PhotoViewer();
```

Left: You can customise which controls are shown in the toolbar

```
<?php
    require "./scripts/common.php";
    $images = getImagesInPath
    ("images/nature");
    foreach ($images as $image)
    {
        echo "slideshow.add('$image');
        \n";
    }
?>
</script>
```

This PHP script reuses the `getImagesInPath()` function from common.php. Give it the name of a folder, and it returns a list of the paths of all image files found. It's easy to loop through all the image paths, adding each one to the slideshow. When this page is viewed in a browser, the HTML page will look like simple.html, but there's no need to type in all the image paths.

In the PHP version, the images are shown in alphanumerical order according to their filename. To control the sort order, name your images with a numeric prefix such as 01-, 02-, 03-. This way, you can make sure the photos appear in the order you want.

HotScripts Other free scripts

There are thousands of other scripts you can use to spice up your website. A great resource can be found at www.hotscripts.com. Scripts are categorised by type, and include Ajax, JavaScript and PHP, among others. Most are free to use, so it's simply a matter of searching through the listings to find what you're after.

For example, if you want text to appear on a page letter by letter, so it looks like someone is typing it, try downloading Typewriter Ticker 2.0. This free piece of JavaScript works on many browsers and operating systems.

Resizing images using PHP

Resizing images to upload to your website is one of the most time-consuming tasks in web development, but a simple PHP script can help

ESSENTIALS ●●●

SKILL LEVEL
Beginner
Intermediate
Expert

HOW LONG
2-3 hours

When creating your website, you'll find you need at least two sizes for each image – a thumbnail and a larger version – and possibly more, if you want to change the sizes of any images or add a medium-sized thumbnail. Resizing every image manually would be so tedious that it's tempting not to bother. However, with the help of a little PHP scripting, you can quickly modify existing images and create new ones.

We've already explained how PHP can be used to show random images (page 125) and automate the creation of slideshows on your website (page 128). This is the most common way to use PHP – small scripts that are inserted into HTML files. Here we'll show you how to use PHP to produce images instead of HTML documents. PHP allows this through the use of values known as headers, interpreted by the web browser.

UNDERSTANDING HEADERS
When you view a website, your browser downloads many files from a web server; these are a combination of HTML, CSS and image files. You may be thinking each file is downloaded and opened in the same way that you would open a file from the hard disk on your PC, but it's actually more complicated. Each file that's downloaded

Right: This photo has been resized from 1,500x1,000 pixels to 500x500 pixels

is composed of two parts: a header section that gives the browser information about the file, and a body section with the content, such as the HTML text or an image.

One special header, known as the content type header, tells the browser what type of file it is downloading. For a simple HTML page, the content type is set to 'text/html', which instructs the browser to treat the file as an HTML document. This header is set by the web server, with the decision based on file extension, so .jpg files are assigned the content type 'image/jpeg' and .css files 'text/css'. By default, PHP pages are given a content type of 'text/html' as they are used to make web pages. To produce images, set the content type to 'image/jpeg' and the browser will know to display the file properly.

AUTOMATIC SCALING
PHP can be a big time-saver when scaling images. If you need to alter the sizes of multiple images on your site, just edit the HTML and the image sizes will be updated automatically. Create a PHP script called scale.php and place it anywhere on your website. Rather than creating a separate script for each image to be scaled, we'll show you how to create a single script that accepts parameters for the name of the file to scale, and the size to scale to.

In PHP, information can be passed to scripts by appending parameters to the URL of the PHP script. We can pass three parameters to the scaling script with a URL that looks like this:

```
scale.php?image=garden.jpg&width=
  100&height=100
```

The three parameters are called `image`, `width` and `height`. The first is written with a question mark after the PHP filename; each subsequent one is separated with an ampersand (&). These parameters are enough to write a generic script that can scale an image, identified by the filename after `image=`, to a size specified by the `width` and `height` parameters. The first part of the script is:

```php
<?php
  require_once "common.php";

  $image = $_GET["image"];
  $width = $_GET["width"];
  $height = $_GET["height"];
```

This script is going to produce an image, not text, so it must start with the `<?php` tag that identifies a block of PHP code. The script includes common.php – a script with reusable functions – and then reads the request parameters. This is known as a GET request, which is why the parameters are read from a variable called GET.

The next step is to read the input image and work out how big it is, in order to determine how to scale it down to the requested size:

```php
$size = getimagesize($image);
$original_width = $size[0];
$original_height = $size[1];

if (($original_width <= $width) &&
 ($original_height <= $height) ) {
  $output_width = $original_width;
  $output_height = $original_height;
} else {
  $x_ratio = $width / $original_width;
  $y_ratio = $height / $original_
   height;
  $scale_factor = min($x_ratio, $y_
   ratio);
  $output_width = $scale_factor *
   $original_width;
  $output_height = $scale_factor *
   $original_height;
}
```

The script checks to see if the original image is smaller than the size to which we're trying to scale. If it is, it outputs the original instead of scaling it up, to prevent degradation in quality. The scaling factor is worked out by dividing the original width and height by the desired width and height, then picking the smaller of the two. This allows us to resize the image while maintaining its aspect ratio. When we have the factor, we multiply it by the original dimensions to calculate the output size.

The next part of the script is:

```php
header("Content-type: image/jpeg");
cacheHeaders(30);

$src = imagecreatefromjpeg ($image);
$dst = imagecreatetruecolor($output_
```

width, $output_height);
imageantialias ($dst, true);

```php
imagecopyresampled($dst, $src, 0, 0, 0,
 0, $output_width, $output_height,
 $original_width, $original_height);
imagejpeg($dst);
```

The first two lines set up the headers, telling the browser there is a JPEG coming and that it's cacheable. Caching improves performance by allowing the browser to keep a copy, rather than forcing the script to create a new image the next time the page is viewed. After reading the original image and setting up a blank output image, we call `imagecopyresampled()` to copy and scale the image. Calling `imageantialias()` turns on anti-aliasing, which produces smoother thumbnails.

The final call to `imagejpeg()` sends the resulting image to the web browser. The script can now be called from an HTML page using a normal image tag such as:

```html
<img src="scale.php?image=holiday.
 jpg&width=500&height=500">
```

Above: The single flower.jpg photo has been resized to four different resolutions in the same web page

TIP
Click through to www. redcotbarn.co.uk/ advancedprojects/ php-images to see this PHP script in action.

Creating boxes with round corners

Curved box corners are a stylish design touch, but tricky to perfect. Here we show you a couple of ways to bend those boxes into shape

A smart way to improve your website's design is to add curved edges to any boxes that you might have. However, this is a lot easier said than done, because there's no standard way to add curves in HTML. Fortunately, you can manipulate the corners of boxes using Cascading Style Sheets (CSS), which we covered in detail in Chapter 4. There are a couple of methods you can try, each of which has its own advantages and disadvantages. It's up to you to decide which method you prefer to use in your designs.

If you've read Chapter 4, you'll know that using CSS to separate the design of your website from the HTML code means that you can easily update the look and feel of your site. What's more, CSS simplifies the design process. Without CSS, the only way for you to draw a box with curved edges is by using a table and creating images of curved corners in the top-left, top-right, bottom-left and bottom-right cells. Using a table does work, but it takes a lot of code, is hard to read and difficult to update.

LEARNING CURVE
The first method for drawing curved boxes in CSS requires us to define our stylesheet to include the necessary images for the corners. Instead of using a table for the layout, you should use the `<div>` tag. This defines a section of a web page – in this case, a box.

First, you'll need to create the image files for the rounded corners, making each corner the same colour as the box you want, with the same background colour as your web page. You could use an image editor to create curved boxes, from which you copy and paste the corners into four separate images, but we've created a PHP script to do it automatically. It works by reading request parameters for the style of corner and creating images. The script can be called using this format:

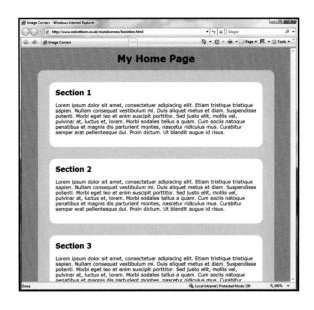

Left: Using CSS allows you to create a set style for boxes that can be applied time and again

Right: These two boxes may look identical, but the top one has been created using PNG images for the corners, whereas JavaScript was used to create the bottom box

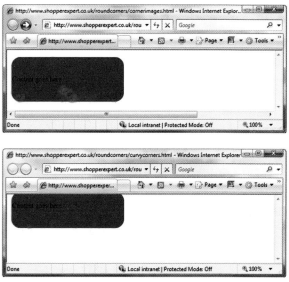

```
round-corner.php?colour=FF0000&background
  =FFFFFF&width=50&height=50&corner=tr
```

The `colour`, `background`, `width` and `height` parameters should be self explanatory. The `corner` parameter specifies which type of corner image will be created. We can use `tr` for top right, `tl` for top left, `bl` for bottom left and `br` for bottom right. You can download the source files, including this PHP script (round-corner.php), from www.redcotbarn.co.uk/advancedprojects/roundcorners by clicking on 'Download sample files'. Click on the 'Round corners using PHP' link to see this script being used in a web page. You'll notice the corner images have jagged edges. This is because the PHP ellipse drawing functions don't support anti-aliasing.

However, there are other ways to draw ellipses, including this one from http://personal.3d-box.com. By replacing the call to `imagefilledellipse()` with `imagefilledellipse_aa()` that we've included for you in common.php, you can get lovely smooth corner images. Click on 'Round corners with anti-aliasing using PHP' at our website to see the difference for yourself.

You can also click on 'Corners using images' to see an example that creates a red box using the top-left.png, top-right.png, bottom-left.png and bottom-right.png files. First, the HTML file defines the CSS:

```
.round-box {
  width: 250px;
  background-color: red;
}
.round-top {
  background: url(top-right.png)
    no-repeat top right;
}
.round-bottom {
  background: url(bottom-right.png)
    no-repeat top right;
}
.corner {
  width: 20px;
  height: 20px;
  border: none;
  display: block;
}
```

You can only define the top-right and bottom-right images in CSS classes. You can add the extra images and `<div>` sections in the HTML:

```
<div class="round-box">
  <div class="round-top">
    <img src="top-left.png"
      class="corner">
  </div>
```

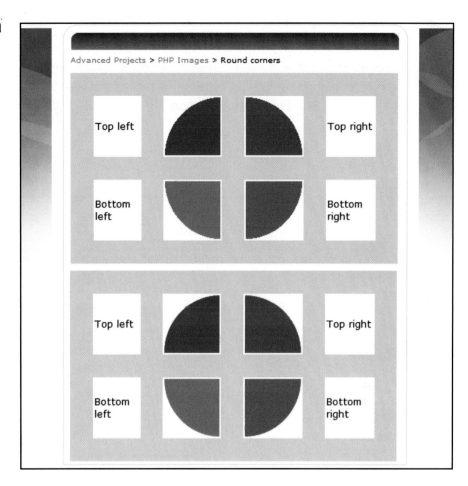

Advanced Projects > PHP Images > Round corners

Above: The top set of corners were generated using PHP. You can see that they're jagged, but it's possible to use alternative drawing methods to produce smooth versions, like those at the bottom

```
  <p>content goes here</p>
<div class="round-bottom">
  <img src="bottom-left.png"
  class="corner">
  </div>
</div>
```

This code creates a box with the properties and colours defined in the round-box class. Inside this, it creates another `<div>` section that uses the round-top class to display the top-right image. Inside this box, a standard HTML `<img>` tag is used to display the top-left image using the attributes in the corner class. The content appears inside the main box. The code uses a similar method for the bottom-right and bottom-left images by creating another box for these two corners.

This method will work with most web browsers. You can put boxes within boxes and create fancier corners simply by changing the corner images. Click on the 'Boxes in boxes' and 'Fancy corners' links on our website to see examples of what can be achieved.

AUTOMATIC CORNERS
Although creating the individual corner images certainly works, you can do the job automatically using the excellent curvyCorners JavaScript library. You can

TIP
You can see each of these examples on our website at www. redcotbarn.co.uk. Dedicated web hosting is not required for this project.

```
var _settings = {
  tl: { radius: 20 },
  tr: { radius: 20 },
  bl: { radius: 20 },
  br: { radius: 20 },
  antiAlias: true,
  autoPad: true
}
var _myBox = new curvyCorners(_
  settings, "rounded-box");
_myBox.applyCornersToAll();
}
</script>
```

This creates a variable called _settings that is used to store the settings, including the radius of each corner in pixels. Setting antiAlias to true makes the curves look smoother, although they take longer to draw. The variable _myBox is an object that draws curves according to the parameters in the _settings variable and with the rounded-box class. The last line tells the script to draw a curved box every time it sees the rounded-box class.

Drawing a curved box is now easy. In the <body> part of the HTML document, you can use:

```
<div class="rounded-box">
  <p>Content goes here.</p>
</div>
```

The beauty of this method is that it can be expanded to draw curved boxes around other classes. Create a new variable with the same settings, but a different class name:

```
var _yournewvariable  = new curvy
  Corners(_settings, "yourclassname");
```

This can be applied to all matching classes by using:

```
_yournewvariable.applyCornersToAll();
```

GOING ROUND THE BEND

Both methods shown here have their strengths, but in most cases it's easier to use JavaScript as it doesn't require you to make the corner images first. We'd suggest that you use the image method only if you fancy corners such as those used in the image below.

Top: Using JavaScript, it's easy to create curved boxes within other curved boxes

Bottom: Corner images can be as fancy as you like and they don't have to be a simple curve

download this free of charge from www.curvycorners.net. Just click on the Download tab and download the .zip file of the latest version. You'll need to extract the rounded_corners_lite.inc.js file. Go to www.redcotbarn.co.uk/advancedprojects/roundcorners and click on the 'Boxes with Javascript corners' link to see this in action.

First, the JavaScript library must be included in the <head> section of the HTML document with the line <script type="text/Javascript" src="rounded_corners_lite.inc.js"></script> (change the path to this file to store it elsewhere). Next, define the rounded-box class in the <style> section:

```
.rounded-box {
  width: 250px;
  background-color: red;
  padding: 10px;
}
```

This is standard CSS for defining an element that is 250 pixels wide with a red background. You must also define the JavaScript that draws the curved lines automatically:

```
<script type="text/JavaScript">
  window.onload = function()
  {
```

Lorem ipsum dolor sit amet, consectetuer adipiscing elit. Etiam tristique tristique sapien. Nullam consequat vestibulum mi. Duis aliquet metus et diam. Suspendisse potenti. Morbi eget leo et enim suscipit porttitor. Sed justo elit, mollis vel, pulvinar at, luctus et, lorem. Morbi sodales tellus a quam. Cum sociis natoque penatibus et magnis dis parturient montes, nascetur ridiculus mus. Curabitur semper erat pellentesque dui. Proin dictum. Ut blandit augue id risus.

Embedding Google Maps on your site

Using Google Maps and some JavaScript, you can add a fully customised interactive map to your site to help your visitors get their bearings

ESSENTIALS ●●●

SKILL LEVEL
Beginner
Intermediate
Expert

HOW LONG
2 hours

Below: This is all the code needed to show a Google Map on a web page

Google Maps (http://maps.google.co.uk) is more than just a website that shows maps. It's a fully customisable application that you can embed in your own website. By using the Google Maps JavaScript application programming interface (API), you can add maps to any web page, which can then be viewed in a normal web browser without requiring extra plug-ins. Using the Google Maps API, you can easily create annotated maps with information such as the location of your holiday home, travel directions, favourite places to hang out and anything else you can imagine.

JavaScript is a lightweight programming language that can be used to add interactivity to HTML pages. All modern web browsers support it. The JavaScript is stored separately from the HTML in files with a .js extension. This helps to keep your website presentation separate from the JavaScript code, and enables you to use the same functions in multiple HTML files without having to duplicate the code.

JavaScript files can be included in your HTML pages by using the script tag `<script src="test.js" type="text/javascript"></script>`. This should be placed in the `<head>` section of the HTML. Alternatively, place the JavaScript code directly inside the `<script>` and `</script>` tags in the `<head>` section, as we've done in this project.

MAP READING

The Google Maps API is divided into four main sections: map objects, events, controls and overlays.

---

simple[1] - Notepad

File   Edit   Format   View   Help

```
<!DOCTYPE html PUBLIC "-//W3C//DTD XHTML 1.0 Strict//EN" "http://www.w3.org/TR/xhtml1/DTD/xhtml1-strict.dtd">
<html xmlns="http://www.w3.org/1999/xhtml">
  <head>
    <meta http-equiv="content-type" content="text/html; charset=utf-8"/>
    <title>Simple Map</title>
    <script src="http://maps.google.com/maps?file=api&amp;v=2&amp;key=lzT34RA" type="text/javascript"></script>
    <script type="text/javascript">

    function load()
    {
      if (GBrowserIsCompatible())
      {
        var map = new GMap2(document.getElementById("map"));
        map.setCenter(new GLatLng(51.500789, -0.142264), 13);
      }
    }

    </script>
  </head>
  <body onload="load()" onunload="GUnload()">
    <div id="map" style="width: 500px; height: 300px"></div>
  </body>
</html>
```

Map objects are the JavaScript objects that represent the map and essentials such as the coordinate system. Events enable the map to respond to user interaction from the mouse and keyboard; they allow the map to pan when you click and drag the mouse, for example. Controls refer to the map controls used to pan and zoom, as well as other controls that can alter the type of map being viewed, such as satellite images. Overlays represent things that are shown onscreen, such as the map image itself. The Overlays section covers other things, such as lines, markers and informational windows such as speech bubbles.

The API allows you to fully customise a Google map. Just about everything can be altered, down to the content of the map itself. We can only cover the basics here, but a full reference for the Google Maps API can be found at http://code.google.com/apis/maps/documentation.

WORKING WITH THE API

The following script tag enables you to include the Google Maps API in an HTML web page:

```
<script src="http://maps.google.com/
maps?file=api&amp;v=2&amp;key=<your
key>" type="text/javascript"></script>
```

Once this script tag is in your HTML page, you'll have access to the API. The screen on page 138 shows an example that places a basic map into an HTML page. You can see a function that loads the map in the `<head>` section with another set of script tags.

First, the `load()` function checks that the current web browser is compatible with the Google Maps API. All modern web browsers are supported, but this ensures that the web page can respond to older web browsers without showing any errors. The second line creates a variable called `map`. This contains a GMap2 object, which is the core object that represents the map.

The map is created by passing a reference to the `div` (a structural HTML element) that will hold it (described in the `<body>` section). The `div` is referenced by using the `document.getElementById()` method, which gets elements in the HTML document by their ID attributes. The final line uses the `setCenter` function on the new map object to set the point at which the map is centred using a latitude and longitude coordinate. Don't worry where the values (51.500789, -0.142264) come from just yet. The parameter to `setCenter` sets the map zoom level from 0 (far out) to 20 (close in).

Next, you'll need to include the load function and create an area in the HTML page where you can place the map; this is shown between the `<body>` tags at the bottom of the screen opposite. The `<body>` tag uses two JavaScript event handlers that are used to manage the map. The `onload` attribute calls the JavaScript function that will create the map and which will be run when the

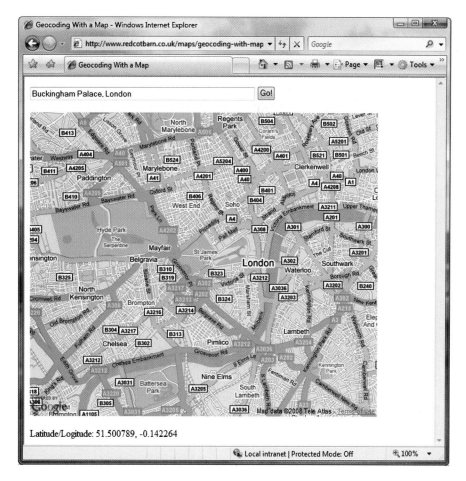

Latitude/Logitude: 51.500789, -0.142264

HTML page is loaded. The `onunload` attribute is used to call `GUnload()` – defined by Google – which releases all memory used by the map when either the web browser is closed or a different HTML page is viewed. This is very important; if you don't call `GUnload()` then the resources used by the map won't be released and the web browser will gradually get slower, until it runs out of memory.

The `<div>` tag marks an area of the page that is to be filled by the map. Its ID needs to match the reference used by `document.getElementByID`, which was used earlier. Using CSS you can specify that the map should be 500 pixels high and 300 pixels wide. You can change these values as necessary. You can also use CSS rules to set where the map appears on the page.

If you go to www.redcotbarn.co.uk/advancedprojects/maps/simple.html, you'll see a map that's centred on Buckingham Palace. The map acts just like any other Google map, so you can click the map and drag it around, for example.

ADDING CONTROLS

The full Google Maps service has a scaling and positioning toolbar. This is disabled by default, but can be shown by adding the following line to the `load()` function in the code opposite:

Above: On our website, click the 'Geocoding with a map' link in the Advanced Projects section to type in a location and see its longitude and latitude displayed

> **TIP**
> Before you can use Google Maps on your site, you need to request a key from http://code.google.com/apis/maps/signup.html. This key is registered to a domain name and helps Google to track usage statistics and prevent abuse of the service.

```
map.addControl(new GLargeMapControl())
```

Other controls can also be added, many of which you'll see if you visit the website at http://maps.google.co.uk. These include `GSmallMapControl`, which creates a smaller control with no zooming slider bar, `GOverviewMapControl`, which adds an overview map to the bottom right-hand corner of the main map, `GSmallZoomControl`, which contains the zoom controls, and `GScaleControl`, which adds a scale legend that updates automatically when you zoom in or out. Furthermore, the scroll wheel on the mouse can be made to control the zoom level of the map using `map.enableScrollWheelZoom()`.

Below: This is the code used to display the map in the screenshot shown on page 139

All these controls have default layout positions that are the same as those on Google Maps, but you can override the defaults and put them anywhere you like.

UPDATING LOCATIONS

Once you've got a map that can be controlled, you need to be able to update its starting location. This is done by changing the coordinates in the `GLatLng()` function. To work out the latitude and longitude coordinates of an address, we use a process called geocoding. Google provides a function to do this in its API, and we've implemented a version of it in the example below. It takes an address that you type in and displays a map of the location, along with the latitude

```
geocoding-with-map[1] - Notepad

File  Edit  Format  View  Help

<!DOCTYPE html PUBLIC "-//W3C//DTD XHTML 1.0 Strict//EN" "http://www.w3.org/TR/xhtml1/DTD/xhtml1-strict.dtd">
<html xmlns="http://www.w3.org/1999/xhtml">
  <head>
    <meta http-equiv="content-type" content="text/html; charset=utf-8"/>
    <title>Geocoding With a Map</title>
    <script src="http://maps.google.com/maps?file=api&amp;v=2&amp;key=1zT34RA" type="text/javascript"></script>
    <script type="text/javascript">

    var map = null;
    var geocoder = null;

    function load()
    {
      if (GBrowserIsCompatible())
      {
        map = new GMap2(document.getElementById("map"));
        map.setCenter(new GLatLng(51.500789, -0.142264), 13);

        geocoder = new GClientGeocoder();
      }
    }

    function findAddress(anAddress)
    {
      if (geocoder)
      {
        geocoder.getLatLng(anAddress, function(aPoint)
        {
          if (!aPoint)
          {
            alert("Sorry, can't locate [" + anAddress + "]");
          }
          else
          {
            map.setCenter(aPoint, 13);
            var elem = document.getElementById("latLng");
            elem.innerHTML = aPoint.lat() + ", " + aPoint.lng();
          }
        });
      }
    }

    </script>
  </head>
  <body onload="load()" onunload="GUnload()">
    <form action="#" onsubmit="findAddress(this.address.value); return false">
      <p>
        <input type="text" size="60" name="address" value="Buckingham Palace, London" />
        <input type="submit" value="Go!" />
      </p>
      <div id="map" style="width: 600px; height: 500px"></div>
      <p>Latitude/Logitude: <span id="latLng">51.500789, -0.142264</span></p>
    </form>
  </body>
</html>
```

and longitude at the bottom. Once you have the coordinates of your chosen location, you can enter these into the `setCenter` function.

CUSTOMISING YOUR MAP

Positioning the map is just the beginning. To make it really useful, you'll want to place markers to highlight specific locations, such as your house. Once you know the latitude and longitude coordinates for all the locations, this task is easy. Just use the following code in the `load()` function after the `setCenter()` line:

```
var latLng = new GLatLng(51.500789,
 -0.142264);
var marker = new GMarker(latLng);
map.addOverlay(marker);
```

This places a marker on the map, where Buckingham Palace is. You can add as many markers as you like, but you need to use new variable names, such as `latLng2` and `marker2`, `latLang3` and `marker3`.

You can then add information windows to the markers that look like speech bubbles, which are activated when the user clicks on a marker. These windows can contain any HTML you like, including pictures and links to other websites. Here is the important section:

```
var latLng = new GLatLng(51.500789,
 -0.142264);
var marker = new GMarker(latLng);
GEvent.addListener(marker, "click",
 function()
{
  marker.openInfoWindowHtml("<p>
    Buckingham Palace</p></p>London
    </p>");
});
map.addOverlay(marker);
```

`GEvent.addListener` is used to 'listen' for a mouse click on the specified marker. When the user clicks on the marker, the inner function is executed, causing an information window to be opened. You can have only one information window open at a time, but you can provide one information window for each marker.

GOING FURTHER

This has been a quick overview of the Google Maps API, but there's plenty more to explore. As we have said, every part of the API is customisable. You can change the appearance of all the controls and use custom images for the markers. On the simpler side, the GDirections utility provides driving instructions for navigating between two locations; this function is used for the gadget we showed you how to use on page 103. Still, you should now be able to create some impressive additions to your website.

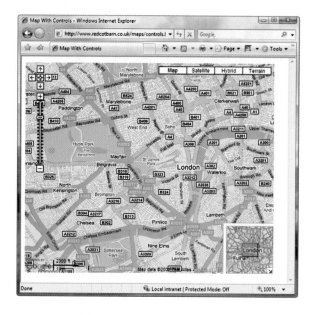

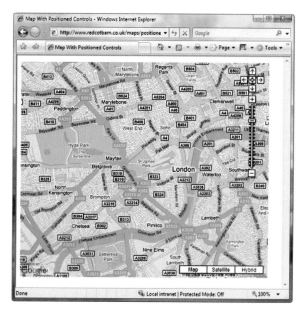

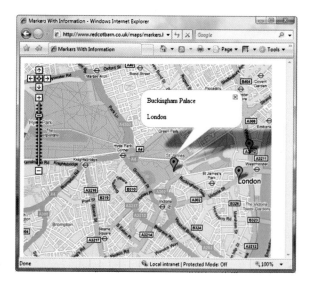

Right: Here we can see the map with its standard controls (top), the thumbnail disabled and the controls repositioned (middle), and the marker and information bubble highlighted (bottom)

Glossary

The language of the web can be impenetrable at times. Here we explain the meanings behind the jargon and the acronyms

Alt tags Text included in an HTML `<img>` tag to be displayed in place of an image when it can't be displayed, or when the mouse is hovered over it.

Bandwidth The amount of data that can be transferred in a specified amount of time. With websites, this tends to refer to the amount of data that can be uploaded and downloaded per month.

Body Everything within the `<body>` section of an HTML page is displayed in a web browser.

Blog Short for web log, a blog is a regularly updated website that usually contains diary entries or news stories.

Broken link A link on a web page that, when clicked on, leads to an error message because the destination page does not exist.

Browser An application used to view web pages. The most popular is Microsoft Internet Explorer, but Mozilla Firefox and Apple Safari are significant others.

Compression Storing data in a format that uses less disk space and bandwidth. Image files are typically compressed to make them around a tenth of their original size.

CSS Cascading Style Sheets provide more control over layout than HTML. When you use CSS, you can make a single change that automatically updates every web page on your site.

Directory See Folder.

Domain name A unique address for a website. The domain name includes everything up to the .com or other extension; for example, www.redcotbarn.co.uk.

Download Transfer of a file from a website to your computer's hard disk.

Dynamic Refers to any interactive parts of a website, such as a Google Map or a YouTube video, where visitors can control the object's behaviour.

Folder A named container on your hard disk that stores a collection of files.

FTP File Transfer Protocol. An FTP application allows you to upload your website from your hard disk to your web-hosting provider's server.

GIF Graphics interchange format. An image format similar to PNG, which is well suited to logos, icons or images with only a small number of colours.

Head The top section of an HTML page, which gives the web browser information about how the page should be displayed, along with links to related CSS files. This can also contain meta tags.

Hits The number of times a web page is visited, measured by tools such as Google Analytics.

Host see Web-hosting provider.

HTML The language that web browsers use to interpret how pages should be displayed.

HTTP HyperText Transfer Protocol. A set of rules that are used to transfer files from web servers to web browsers.

Hyperlink see Link.

JavaScript A scripting – or programming – language that provides a way to produce dynamic content on a web pages.

JPG or **JPEG** Joint Photographic Experts Group Format. The most common image format used on the internet, usually used for photos.

Keywords Search terms entered into a search engine to locate relevant websites. These words should be used as meta tags on web pages to improve search rankings.

Link A page element that, when clicked on, takes the visitor to another page in your site or an external website.

Menu See Navigation bar.

Meta tag A keyword that describes the content of a web page, stored in the `<head>` section of each HTML file. Meta tags can be used by search engines as part of the ranking process, which determines how relevant a website is to a user's search.

MP3 One of the most common audio formats used on the internet, and compatible with virtually all computers and audio players.

MySQL An open-source database management system. It uses the SQL programming language to add, remove and modify information in the database.

Navigation bar A set of links that help visitors navigate to the main sections of your website. Navigation bars are commonly placed across the top of the page, vertically on the left-hand side and across the bottom of a web page.

Open source Any program for which the source code – the collection of human-readable files that are converted into a computer-executable format – is made publicly available for use or modification.

PHP Recursive acronym that stands for hypertext preprocessor. PHP is a web-scripting language which is typically used to produce HTML web pages, but can also produce images.

PNG Portable Network Graphic. An image format originally designed as an alternative to GIF. Unlike GIF, animation is not supported, but like GIF, PNG files don't lose any data when compressed.

Podcast An audio version of a blog. Podcasts are usually relatively short radio-style clips that contain spoken information or entertainment, which can include music.

Resolution The resolution of a monitor is measured in pixels. A typical resolution is 1,024x768, which refers to the number of horizontal and vertical pixels respectively.

RSS feeds An RSS feed is a regularly updated information source that tells RSS reader programs about new blog posts, news stories or podcasts that are available on a certain website.

Scripts Short pieces of programming code that perform actions on a web page. Scripts can include code written in programming languages including Java, PHP, Perl, CGI, ASP and others.

Search engine optimisation Usually referred to as SEO, this is the technique or techniques used to increase a website's ranking on a search engine.

Server space The storage for websites provided by web-hosting companies.

Site map An ordered set of text links that lists all the pages on a website in one convenient place.

SSL Secure sockets layer. An encryption technology used for ensuring the security of data sent across the internet.

Streaming Content such as video or audio that is viewed by a user while it is being delivered to them over an internet or network connection.

Subdomain Some web hosts allow you to create several separate websites using similar domain names to your main website. For example, a subdomain of www.eppingkarate.co.uk could be www.members.eppingkarate.co.uk.

Thumbnail A small image or photograph, which can usually be clicked on to see a larger version.

TLD Top-level domain. This is the final part of a website's URL. Examples include .com, .co.uk, .org, .gov.uk, .net and many others.

Traffic The number of visitors to a website.

Upload The process of copying your website files from your hard disk to your web host's servers.

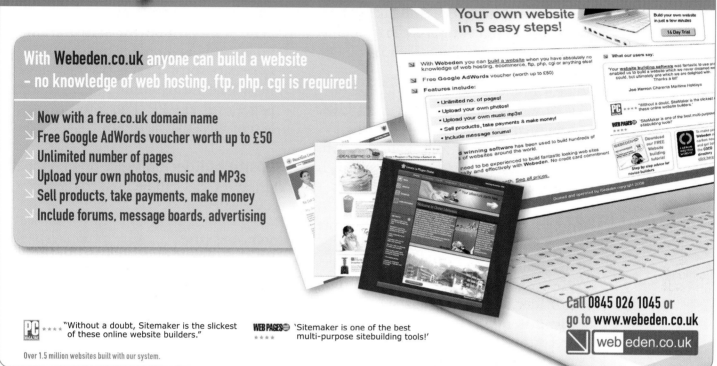

URL Uniform resource locator. This is the unique address of every page on the web. For example, www.bbc.co.uk is unique to the BBC's homepage, while www.redcotbarn.co.uk/directions/index.html will take you straight to Redcot Barn's Driving Directions page.

Visitor Someone arriving at a page on your website either by typing its URL into their web browser or clicking a link from another website or a search engine. Used interchangeably with user and reader.

Web Short for World Wide Web. Invented in 1990 by Sir Tim Berners-Lee.

Web-hosting provider A service provider that stores your website on its server to make it constantly available to visitors. Other services, such as email, can also be included.

Web page An HTML document that forms part of a website.

Web-safe colours Not all web browsers can display all colours, but most support a standardised selection of 256 colours. Using only web-safe colours ensures your website will be correctly displayed since, if a browser cannot display any of the colours you chose, it will display alternatives.

Web server A computer that runs the necessary software and has the networking capabilities to deliver web pages over HTTP. The software used is typically Apache or IIS.

Website builder Software or an online program that can be used to create a website.

WYSIWYG What you see is what you get. A WYSIWYG editor is one that allows you to create web pages in a graphical form, much like desktop publishing software. It converts the pages you create into the required HTML code automatically.

XML Xtensible Markup Language. Similar to HTML but, instead of describing the content of a web page, XML describes the content in terms of what data is being described.

BUILD A BETTER WEBSITE

EDITORIAL
Editor
Jim Martin
jim_martin@dennis.co.uk
Production Editor
Janey Goulding
Art Editor
Anand Parmar
Cover illustration
MagicTorch

CONTRIBUTORS
Gareth Beach, Steve Haines, Emily Hodges, James Lumgair, David McKinnon, Mike Mosedale, Matt Preston, Julian Prokaza, Nik Rawlinson, Matthew Sparkes, Dave Stevenson

PHOTOGRAPHY
Danny Bird, Hugh Threlfall, Linda Duong

ADVERTISING
Julie Price
jullie_price@dennis.co.uk
Andrea Mason
andrea_mason@dennis.co.uk

INTERNATIONAL LICENSING
The content in this bookazine is available for international licensing overseas.
Contact Winnie Liesenfeld +44 20 7907 6134, winnie_liesenfeld@dennis.co.uk

MANAGEMENT
Bookazine Manager
Dharmesh Mistry (020 7907 6100, dharmesh_mistry@dennis.co.uk)
Publishing Director
John Garewal
Operations Director
Robin Ryan
MD Advertising
Julian Lloyd-Evans

Circulation Director
Martin Belson
Finance Director
Brett Reynolds
Group Finance Director
Ian Leggett
Chief Executive
James Tye
Chairman
Felix Dennis

A DENNIS PUBLICATION
Dennis Publishing, 30 Cleveland Street, London W1T 4JD. Company registered in England. All material © Dennis Publishing Limited, licensed by Felden 2008, and may not be reproduced in whole or part without the consent of the publishers.

Dennis Publishing operates an efficient commercial reprints service. For more details, please call 020 7907 6667.

LIABILITY
While every care was taken during the production of this bookazine, the publishers cannot be held responsible for the accuracy of the information or any consequence arising from it. Dennis Publishing takes no responsibility for the companies featured in this bookazine.

Printed by Benham Goodhead Print (BGP).

The paper used within this bookazine is produced from sustainable fibre, manufactured by mills with a valid chain of custody.

ISBN 1-906372-19-5

recycle
When you have finished with this magazine please recycle it.